Copyright (C) Michelle Garrett-Chambers. All rights reserved.

No part of this publication shall be reproduced, transmitted, or sold in whole or in part in any form without prior written consent of the author, except as provided by the United States of America copyright law. Any unauthorized usage of the text without express written permission of the publisher is a violation of the author's copyright and is illegal and punishable by law. All trademarks and registered trademarks appearing in this guide are the property of their respective owners.

For permission requests, write to the publisher, addressed "Attention: Permissions Coordinator," at the address below.

Publish Your Purpose
141 Weston Street, #155
Hartford, CT, 06141

The opinions expressed by the Author are not necessarily those held by Publish Your Purpose.

Ordering Information: Quantity sales and special discounts are available on quantity purchases by corporations, associations, and others. For details, contact the author at hello@benourished.im

Edited by: Lily Capstick
Cover design by: Michelle Garrett-Chambers
Typeset by: Michelle Garrett-Chambers

ISBN: 979-8-88797-148-3 (hardcover)
ISBN: 979-8-88797-147-6 (paperback)
ISBN: 979-8-88797-149-0 (ebook)

Library of Congress Control Number: 2024946043

First edition, November 2024

The information contained within this book is strictly for informational purposes. The material may include information, products, or services by third parties. As such, the Author and Publisher do not assume responsibility or liability for any third-party material or opinions. The publisher is not responsible for websites (or their content) that are not owned by the publisher. Readers are advised to do their own due diligence when it comes to making decisions.

Publish Your Purpose is a hybrid publisher of non-fiction books. Our mission is to elevate the voices often excluded from traditional publishing. We intentionally seek out authors and storytellers with diverse backgrounds, life experiences, and unique perspectives to publish books that will make an impact in the world. Do you have a book idea you would like us to consider publishing? Please visit PublishYourPurpose.com for more information

Special thanks to **Amore du Plessis Photography** for the gorgeous images of my food.
It was a real joy working together and I'm very much looking forward to creating new dishes for our next photo shoot in the new year!

RISK

And then the day came
when the risk
to remain tight
in a bud
was more painful
than the risk
it took
to blossom.

ANAIS NIN, **1903-1977**

CONTENTS

Part 1: The Beginning

Welcome	1
Food Heart	6

Summary

Food Category Listings	7
Getting Started	9
Well-Being: Mental, Emotional, Physical	11

Part 2: The Detail

Preparation	19
Raw Salad Food Charts	32, 33, 57, 58
Non-Starchy Food Charts	35, 61
Starchy Food Charts	38, 62
Pantry Guide Chart	40, 41

CONTENTS

Part 3: The Shopping Guide

Shopping for Plant-Based Foods — 54

Kitchen Gadgets — 65

Part 4: Final Words

Cheat Food Heart — 80

Gratitude — 81

Copyright — 85

Medical Disclaimer — 86

Author's Recommendations — 87

Part 1
The Beginning

Welcome to KISS! Plant-Based Eating

The SUPER SIMPLE method that guides you from Zero to Plant-Based in as long as it takes you to read this book.

Keeping plant-based eating super simple!

You want to go vegan or plant-based but find that you're stuck; the desire is there but you don't quite know how to get off the starting blocks. There's also the issue of time and money. You're busy with life and genuinely don't have the time for all the research necessary to tell you what to eat and how to cook it. And you think it's likely going to cost you a small fortune.

Often this results in us reaching out for the vegan processed foods or going back to our current diet as it's all we know.
This is a vicious cycle that can be frustrating and disheartening.

I've been in exactly the same spot myself, struggling to understand how to eat plant-based, or even what to buy to get started, but after years of trial and error I accidentally created a very simple solution to the problem.

This book is NOT about how bad your current diet is, nor how good eating plant-based may be. This book has a simple purpose; to help you reach your personal plant-based goals, using a method I created that helped me to successfully reach my own.

With this in mind, let's take a look at what this book IS about. It's simple; it's purpose is to teach you how to eat plant-based effectively and with ease, every day.

Using the book as a guide, you will:

1. Understand ingredients and know what to buy.
2. Understand how to use those ingredients.
3. Enjoy cooking and creating meals that count nutrients not calories.
4. Stick with the new way of eating!

Further, the guide will help you to expand your pantry. Bit by bit, you will be able to replace old, outdated items in place of new and exciting dry store ingredients. Previously, these items would be confusing with their strange names and wondering how to use them but now, they'll have their own dedicated and useful places in your cupboards. I love opening my fridge to be greeted with what looks like a cool garden, brimming with a rainbow of colours from all types of fruits, vegetables, herbs, and salad items. I love the fresh aroma that hits me; I often open the fridge just to look at, and smell, the contents!

Initially, I struggled to eat this way. But, that struggle, along with all my many kitchen 'fails' was the trigger for creating the method that ultimately helped me to succeed on this journey. In the process, my new diet changed so many other facets of my life; glowing skin, leaner body, increased energy being just a few of those benefits.

I call it the "FOOD HEART METHOD"

Once you see it, the **Food Heart** will be self-explanatory. It is a "visual aid" that details what food groups we need to eat each day, together with how much of these foods we need to eat. I have used an 80:20 ratio to help make this method even easier to follow. **Good Food: 80%** Cheat Food: 20%

To help further, I've included a summary of foods within the food heart categories so, when you make out your next shopping list, you'll know at a glance what kinds of ingredients to include.

This is a great way to get you off the starting blocks; from "stuck" to "go." And I think you'll be pleasantly surprised at how effective the food heart method is in helping you to understand how to eat plant-based in a glance.

Instead of counting calories and restricting yourself on things you love, weighing ingredients, or adding up points, with the food heart method you'll be able to eat in abundance till you're fully satisfied with none of the sugar slump and bloated feelings that accompany so many of the processed and refined foods in a standard Western diet, simply by using the food hearts and focusing on the nutrients on your daily plate.

I've covered all I need to at this point, so, let's get you started on this super simple new way of eating!

How the guide works:

We're starting the opposite way around, with the summary placed at the beginning of the book followed with the more in-depth information behind that.

This is because I want you to see the food heart first. That alone will be a full explanation of how a daily food plate needs to be constructed.

I've then followed that up with a summary of foods from each group within the food heart so you have an idea of the types of foods to pick up when you're next out food shopping.

Next, I have included a section on mental well-being activities. Feeding our mind is just as important as feeding the rest of our body. What you choose to put in your mouth has a profound effect on your brain; however, the brain needs more than just food to keep it healthy. It needs stimulation and love from outside sources too.
To finish the summary section, I have included a list of handy-to-have, but not essential, "Kitchen gadgets."

You can use this book in whatever way suits your needs best. Hit the ground running by diving straight into the food heart and the ingredients list or take a more detailed look at it; digest it all a bit more (deliberate pun!) and continue reading from start to finish so you get the whole picture before you dive in.

Further, to help get you started straight away, I've written a set of easy-to-follow, everyday recipes, included as a bonus at the end of this book. Two books in one!

Lastly, and before we get into the nitty gritty of **Kiss!** I want to thank you for purchasing my book. I truly want to inspire and compel you to take the small leap of faith in claiming back control of your diet. Choosing what, and how, you eat is empowering; it's a form of self-love, giving gratitude to your body by way of good nutrition instead of empty calories that ultimately lead to poor health and a shorter life span. Let's do this. Let's **KISS!** it to Plant-Based Eating in as long as it takes you to read this book.

To Your Best Food Choices and Impeccable Health
Keeping it Super Simple
Michelle

Based on the food heart, as illustrated above, the following pages explain in summary how we need to construct our daily food plate, including listings of typical foods from all the components within the food heart.

Summary

Food Heart Category	Daily %
Raw Salad Items	40%–50%
Non-Starchy Vegetables, Greens, and Fruits	30%–40%
Starchy Vegetables, Grains, Beans, and Fruits	10%–20%
Healthy Fats	5%–10%
Sources of dietary fats include whole foods such as avocado, nuts, chia seeds, coconut, flax seeds, nondairy chocolate with 70% or higher content of cocoa, cacao nibs, tofu, edamame (soy) beans, dates, broccoli, tomatoes, raw berries	
Berries *(blueberries, blackberries, strawberries, raspberries etc)*	5%–10%
Nuts and Seeds	5%
A handful of berries plus a palmful of raw nuts, crushed and sprinkled over raw salads is a nice way to jazz up the leaves. Smoothies are another great way to incorporate your daily dose of beautiful berries and nutritious nuts.	
Fruits *(such as apple, banana, pear, mango, pineapple, satsuma, grapes, plums, kiwi fruit, cherries)*	4–5 pieces a day
Ground Flaxseed, Nutritional Yeast Flakes, Ground Chia Seeds	1 tbsp each daily

Incorporate more nutrition on your plate with these helpful tips!

1 Sprinkle a tablespoon of ground flaxseed, nutritional yeast flakes and ground chia seeds on your salads, soups, and fruit bowls, or blended into your daily smoothie or plant-based ice cream.

Include a daily smoothie into your diet; go for a berry-based smoothie one day, ramp it up with a green-based smoothie the next day. Keep alternating as to not get bored and to max out the available nutrients. **2**

3 Ensure that you eat a portion of healthy fats derived from foods such as avocado, raw plant-based chocolate, nuts, and seeds every day.

Bonus Tip:

Soak nuts, seeds, grains and legumes overnight before eating or cooking, then dry off in either a dehydrator or spread out on a tray and place in your oven on the lowest setting possible. The process of soaking will break down the phytic acid and enable your body to fully absorb the nutrients into your bloodstream. Eating without doing this means the body struggles to extract any available nutrients as the phytic acid binds to the intestinal tract making absorption into the body difficult.

Getting Started

A good way to begin this journey is to start with one day a week fully plant-based. As you, and your body, become more accustomed to this way of eating, and invariably start to enjoy it more over time, you'll end up with one day per week of old eating ways and 6 days of plant-based, or like me, 100% plant-based. This is a great goal to work towards!

Aim to build yourself up to at least 80% plant-based over time. Do it in a way that supports your current lifestyle, finances, and demands.

There is no wrong way to do this!
Enjoy the process!

More than anything, this is a journey of discovery for so many things. New foods and flavours, new ways of cooking and eating, new gadgets to play with in the kitchen, a great topic of conversation with friends, family, and colleagues.

You'll be surprised how curious and interested people are when they see you embracing this new lifestyle. Truth be told, most people I speak to really want to embrace these changes. They just struggle to get started.

They, and you, are the very reason I decided to write this book.

"But how can I stay motivated?"

"I always feel so guilty after cheating on my diet..."

You don't have to be perfect

If you have a bad day and you fall off the wagon, we all do, right; it's part of being human, my advice is "stop feeling guilty about it".

Don't beat yourself up over those 20 percent times when you eat the donut or have a cheat night. Over time, those cravings for the old foods do die off. Your taste buds come back to life and you start to find that you crave other foods.

For me, it's spinach and salad. My body loves the nutrients it gets when it's fed them, sending out signals for me to go find a salad bar or buy a bag of greens when it needs that top up.

I never imagined there would ever be a day that I actually craved and was wholly satisfied with salad. But I am and I love it.

Well-Being: Mental, Emotional, Physical

Keep your mental health in mind

Eating well is just one of the ways that we can take care of our mental health. In conjunction with forming better eating habits, we also need to look at forming new daily habits that, when taken as a whole way of life, will work in synergy with eating well.

Self-care and self-love is the greatest gift you can give to yourself

---

You are the most important person there is; remember this every day and give thanks to yourself.

When you love yourself, that love shines through and radiates outwards to those who cross your path. There's nothing nicer than feeling that light energy from someone; receiving a smile and a hello for no apparent reason.

It lifts us and makes us feel good inside. It improves the rest of our day. Working on yourself should become something that you view as necessary and important.

Improving your mental health

You may be thinking, "What steps can I take in improving my mental health?" My response to this is that there are many methods, and they don't need to be costly, time consuming, or complicated. Often, we find the greatest joy in the simplest of acts. Let me share some of the ways that I have used to help benefit my own mental well-being.

Exercise

Dr. Michael Greger of Nutritionfacts.org and bestselling author of **How Not To Die** and **How Not To Diet** advises that we should aim to get 90 mins of vigorous exercise every day. The important bit is to get your heart rate up. Make it vigorous enough so that it is difficult to hold a conversation and so that you sweat and feel out of breath.

If you don't do any exercise at the present time you can start with walking. Ten thousand steps daily is a good way to get started. Once you start counting your steps it becomes quite addictive and you get pleasure from seeing those steps add up each day. Make changes like walking up and down the stairs instead of using the lift or escalator; go for walks on your work breaks; walk after your evening meal or early in the morning. Whatever opportunities you see, grab them!

You'll soon find that it becomes a habit along with your new eating habits. Before long, that walk turns into a jog or even a full-on run. I rediscovered my love of running since changing up my diet. Having not ran for years, I surprised myself with how quickly it came back, and how much I enjoyed it.

Love

Spend as much time as possible in the company of friends and family. This time is priceless for your mental well-being. Love and laughter are as essential to our well-being as food is in keeping us healthy in body and mind. We know from the many lockdowns we all endured during the pandemic years how damaging separation can be; connection and interaction with others is vital. Find beautiful places to explore together—woodlands, parks, beaches, hill walks, coastal paths—soaking up the beauty of the sounds, smells and energy of fresh, clean nature as you go along.

Love yourself

Be it with meditations, enjoying a hobby, going to the gym, having massages, doing voluntary activities such as beach cleans or tree planting, watching anime, or playing with your grandchildren. Whatever it is that makes you feel alive, just do it with no guilt.

Hug

Hard, long, and loving. Every single day. That exchange of positive energy will fill you with happiness and keep you lifted for longer.

Eat well

This is part of your self-love regime. There is no better feeling than the feeling of good health, vitality, and energy that you gain when you eat nutrient rich foods. Your body loves you for it and rewards you with good health and an outward glow that everyone notices.

Give gratitude

Be thankful at the end of every day. No matter what it may have thrown at you; there is always light in the dark.

Tell your people that you love them. And accept love back. We are all deserving of love and kindness and the more we give, the more we receive back in many ways. Give thanks to nature for providing us with all the tools that we need in the form of the widest array of nutrients, many that we have not yet even discovered, that give us the energy and sustenance we need in order to thrive in the greatest of health. And let's make it our mission to take care of this beautiful earth and all that occupy her space as we are, ultimately, all one and the same.

I hope that my summary has been helpful in giving you a quick overview and better understanding of eating plant-based. On the following pages I will go into some greater detail and explain the 3 key areas that we can work on to help us change our relationship with food.

Read on to find out more and see what a huge difference these simple changes can make to your entire life and eating habits.

Happy healthy reading!

Part 2
The Detail

So many names
So much confusion

Plant Based. Vegan*. Vegetarian. Flexitarian. Pescatarian. Raw Vegan. Nutritarian** . . . Carnitarian??? (Is that really a thing??)

For the purposes of this book, and because we like a label for everything we do, we are going with the phrase:

"Plant-Based Nutritarian"

What does that mean?

Plant-Based

Eating foods that have been derived from plants in their natural and unaltered state. From the earth. Not a factory, laboratory, or test tube. Nothing taken away; nothing artificial added.

Nutritarian

A person who eats for the purposes of fulfilling the body's need of essential nutrients in order to sustain optimum health and longevity. Simply put: to eat for nutrition.

Put Together

Eating plant foods that have been derived from the earth in as true to original form as possible. This means in an unaltered, unmodified way and unrefined form. The focus being, to eat high quantities of the thousands of known and unknown nutrients that our bodies need in order to keep us in amazing active and energetic, glowing health well into our 80s, 90s, and even 100s.

I know so many wonderful people who have the greatest desire to eat better and subsequently feel better but, due to the many life pressures, time and money restraints, and so much confusion out there, they literally don't know where to start or even how to continue if they do start. Happily, that's where I can help, using the food heart method I created and that helped me on my own journey to better eating.
After a lot of trial and errors, I'm now a fully-fledged plant-based nutritarian, eating my best life and looking and feeling the benefits of this wonderful way of eating, living and thinking.

Over the years I have studied, listened, researched, and cooked my way to a level of understanding and expertise in the plant eating arena. My learning and research continues, and always will, as more and more is discovered about how we eat, why we are so sick in this modern age, and why eating for nutrition is the only sensible eating habit you should ever embrace.

This too, will be your easiest transition to better eating and your greatest health—looking and feeling better than you could ever have imagined. No more confusion. No more trying and "failing." You can do this with so much ease I guarantee that by the end of this book you'll be a fully-fledged, plant-based nutritarian guru with such a wealth of knowledge and understanding that you'll be scratching your head wondering why you didn't do this sooner.

Let's KISS this!!!!

***Vegan.** Much confusion, surprisingly even amongst professional chefs, lies in the difference between the phrases "plant-based" and "vegan."*
Here is how I define the two:

Vegan *is* **NOT** *a diet. It is an animal rights movement where those who identify as vegan will not eat, wear, or be entertained by anything that has, or may have, somewhere along the chain, harmed or killed any animal.*

Plant-based **IS** *a diet. It is eating foods that have been derived from the whole food with as little change to its original form as is possible. Because the food has not been altered, it retains more of its original, intact nutrients than processed food.*

***Nutritarian.** A phrase I first heard coined by the eminent Dr. Joel Fuhrman, a leading MD, New York Times bestseller and specialist in plant-based health and nutrition. Following years spent reading his many books such as* Super Immunity, Eat to Live, *and* Fast Food Genocide *together with watching multiple hours of his talks and debates, in particular, the* "Real Truth on Health Conference" *series that can be found on Youtube, I devised my simple* **Food Heart Method** *as a fast track to understanding basic nutrition that would assist others in making the change to real health without the confusion or the need to spend years researching and studying. I did that, so you don't have to! With much gratitude to Dr. Joel Fuhrman, whose work in helping others continues. May his message of health and longevity continue to be spread and reach as many people as possible. We all deserve good health, truth, and the knowledge of how to achieve it.*

Preparation is key

A good friend once said to me "PPP = PPP" aka
"P*ss Poor Preparation = P*ss Poor Performance"

I took this to heart; in all its funniness, its the truth. To make any effective change, we must first prepare for it. In order to transition easily from your current diet style to plant-based nutritarian, preparation is needed in the following three key areas:

1. Preparing the Mind
2. Preparing the Kitchen
3. Preparing Your Time

Let me first start with:

Preparing the Mind

This is likely going to be the toughest of the changes you make because the mind is our most powerful tool. So, let's turn that right on its head and embrace the fact that the mind **is** our most powerful and persuasive tool.

You can talk yourself out of, and in to, anything right? Yes!

At this time your mind is full of everything that you've learnt and read about food, diet, and nutrition so far. Whatever age you are, whatever you have learnt, you are capable of unlearning and relearning. We do this all the time.

Therefore, in order to "eat" differently you need to "think" differently.

It's a mindset change. We can use the most powerful tool we have, our mindset, to help us make the changes that are needed to look at, think of, and eat food in a new and ultimately more beneficial way.

The change starts before you even realize it—that first thought is the catalyst that will bring about the changes you desire.

You further imbed that mindset change when you start chatting to your friends and family about wanting to eat better. It may be subtle, so subtle that even you don't notice it at first, but those first thoughts have already started to shift your mindset; you have started to think differently about what you eat and the change has already unconsciously begun.

Taking the first steps in anything is always the hardest. Once the seed is planted in your mind, the struggle then is trying to get off the starting blocks.

At this point, it can get very confusing as you scroll through endless blogs and recipes online, all telling you that you need to change or offering long lists of ingredients in recipes (not before you've read the endless pages of their life story first!) that include items you've never heard of. Even if you knew where to get them, you still wouldn't know how to use them!

Trying to understand what to buy, what to eat, how to cook —it is a challenge in itself on this journey. I found this very hard and, at times, quite frustrating. What could I do with vegetables to make them exciting?! As for eating out, my old café habits were defunct. I found myself disappointed and quite often even annoyed when there was nothing on the menu that I could eat.

In the early years of my transition to plant-based nutritarian, I researched endlessly looking for answers as to what I should be eating; I read so many books (I do now have an impressive library at least!), watched documentaries, and even studied vegan and alkaline nutrition to help my mind understand what it needed me to do to eat well. Although this has taken years to accumulate, it was the best thing I could have done.

At that time, veganism was still under the radar and plant-based was not talked of or even understood. I started to refresh my pantry with new items and began to cook again. It was really like starting from the beginning—as if I'd never cooked before. I was learning about new ingredients and trying to understand how to use them.

There were many disasters, let me tell you! But, over time, things began to fall into place. I began to understand food in a completely different way. I understood why it was necessary to eat the rainbow, so that I obtained the maximum array of nutrients all the colours provided. I understood why I needed a balance of raw and cooked, that green foods are the most nutritionally dense, that steaming is better than boiling, and that oil is no longer necessary and instead can be replaced with water or stock.

Slowly, the disasters began to be less frequent and the successes soon outweighed them. My taste buds came alive again; everything tasted so much fresher and sweeter—apples had never been my favourite fruits but somehow, these little gems tasted so much sweeter and juicier than they had before my transition.

I began to see food in a new way; I understood it. I could see what I needed to do with it, how it should be eaten, how it would react to being steamed or air fried or popped in the dehydrator. My cooking time became a huge passion for me. Using so many new dry store ingredients, spices, and herbs was exciting! I'd always loved cooking before but this was on a whole new level of enjoyment.

It wasn't just the process of creating that gave me happiness; the way I felt after eating blew me away. I had so much energy; no brain fog, no sugar slump in the afternoon; I started to lose weight naturally from around my middle.

You can't underestimate how good that makes you feel. Especially when people around you notice too: "you look great," "your skin is lovely," "tell me your secret, I want to look like you."

Leaner, happier, more energetic

A big change in mindset comes with the knowledge of understanding WHY we need to eat. As silly as this sounds, we have forgotten. Eating has become a more mindless activity due to a greater abundance of foods available at all times of the day and night, all year round. We are naturally built for periods of famine.

In our hunter gatherer days, we would have been well used to going for long periods without food. In our modern times of fast foods, we generally don't experience famine anymore. Unfortunately, the type of foods that we can access all day every day are nutrition-less at best and dangerous at worst.

Ultimately, a continued eating pattern throughout life of nutrition-less processed fast foods results in very poor health, often from around middle age.

Our reason for eating is simple. To provide the cells of our body with the full array of nutrients that it requires in order to work efficiently and keep us in good health for all the decades of our lives.

Instead of eating for this reason, we now eat to fill a "hunger pang" or as a way of socialising, with little thought as to what we eat. As long as it fills the gap, it's fine. We have fallen into a pattern of three meals a day. Cereal or toast for breakfast, sandwiches and crisps for lunch, meat and two vegetables for dinner. Snacks in between and takeaways as treats.

This is your mindset now because it's what you've been taught over the years. It is old thinking. Outdated. And it doesn't work in our best interests as is seen in the poor health of the nation.

Following the food heart method will help you greatly in changing this old mindset and eating pattern as you begin to follow the recommendations it gives to eat mostly raw salad and steamed non starchy foods with the smaller portions of starchy foods, fruits, berries, healthy fats, and so on.

It doesn't take long for the food heart to become your natural way of eating; your new habit and mindset that you don't even think about anymore. My mindset change happened over time. Yours will be a lot quicker because you've got me to help you. I'm passionate about helping people and I believe that we all have a right to the truth and to being healthy. If I couldn't share my own learning with you, my time spent over the years would be pointless.

I first began sharing my knowledge by hosting small "cook and eat workshops" in my local area. I set up in a room that I had to transform into a make-shift kitchen, bringing with me my kitchen gadgets from home and all the ingredients required for a daily nutrient plate.

At the beginning of each workshop, I would give a short talk on eating plant-based and, to help people understand better with a visual, I drew a "food pyramid." That was OK. It was well received and understood. Unfortunately, it didn't look very pretty. I'm not very good at straight-line drawing or writing; I'm more of a curve lover! Hence, the food pyramid was phased out and I created the food heart (see page 10).

The food heart is very simple. On it is everything you need to eat in a day, every day, in order to feed the body with adequate nutrition so it can be kept as healthy and well as possible and support you in your everyday life as you go about your business.

Not only does it tell you what you need to eat daily, it also gives you the visual ratio of each food type so you can now easily balance out your plate to maximise the nutrient intake.

I will take a second here to add that, however well balanced we eat, it is always wise to get a well-woman/well-man check every year and at every age so that you can determine if you are lacking in anything that may require supplementation.

B12, for example, is a very common nutrient that many people lack in, whether or not meat is included in their diet. I am not covering supplements in this book, however, this is just a note so you're aware and alerted to get your levels checked and ensure you aren't deficient in anything vital.

My further recommendation is to do this via your professional and suitably qualified healthcare practitioner. They will know your personal history including any current health issues you may have; they can read your results properly and can also advise you accordingly if you happen to be on other medications. Some supplements can adversely interfere with other prescribed medications. Go get yourself checked out; it's another positive step in helping with your mindset preparation and change because you have made a considered and deliberate decision to take some control of your body and what you choose to put in it. You are also telling yourself that you DO care about yourself and you are consciously now looking after yourself in ways you've likely overlooked previously.

This is the beginning of your mindset change. Just by reading up to here, you have already started preparing your mind to embrace a new way of thinking about food and hence a new way of buying, cooking, and eating.

Congratulations for taking these steps to this point; prepare yourself to feel the most excited about food than you've ever been in your entire life as we take a deeper dive into eating nature's bounty throughout the pages of this book.

Further, what you LEARN here, will be invaluable information that stays with you forever. Who wants to take a few years of their life out & spend a HUGE amount of money to study nutrition when you can get all the essentials in a few pages.

This is where you realise that you've known this stuff all along; the knowledge has just been skewed with far too much conflicting information thrown at you every second of every day, usually in order to persuade you to buy something.

Allow yourself to forget everything you've learnt so far about food and dieting and honour yourself for opening your heart to creating this change in your life and in the lives of those around you.

Your family, friends, and colleagues alike will be wowed by your personal transformation and you will be compelled to share this new love of Food and Self with everyone you know, and even everyone you don't!

Let's take another look at what is about to change your mindset. Go back to the beginning and take another look at that **FOOD HEART**.

Print it out. Stick it on your fridge where you will see it daily. It will soon become second nature to you and, instinctively you will understand WHAT you need to eat and HOW you need to put your food plates together at every single meal.

The food heart is the link between the "mindset prep" and the "kitchen prep." Now that you know HOW to eat, you can start shopping and filling your fridge and pantry knowing WHAT to buy.

Eating in a plant-based nutritarian way really IS super simple; you're already halfway there by getting to this point.

Now that we are getting into the mindset change preparation, let's link in the second change.

Preparing the kitchen

The kitchen change is something that will happen over time as you transition further into your new way of cooking and eating, and as you discover your own ways of doing things.

The first changes I made, and likely you will too, were the contents of my fridge, freezer, and pantry. I replaced old packaged and processed items with fresh whole foods, dry store ingredients, spices, and even new ingredients that I'd previously not heard of!

As for kitchen aids; you will already have several useful gadgets dotted around . Over time, as you delve deeper into cooking without oils and using ingredients in a different way, you will add a few more. The key point is, you don't need a huge arsenal of complicated or expensive gadgets to get going.

On the following pages, I've drawn up some easy-to-follow charts that break down the food heart. They specify some good examples of foods that will come under 'raw salad' 'starchy' 'non-starchy' and so on. See pages 32-33, 35, 38 and 40-41 for quick reference. You can get a head start on making some early kitchen changes now with the help of the charts!

Let's start with the biggest proportion food group that will make up at least 40% to 50% of your daily intake:

 ## Raw Salad - Aim for 40%

By far the food that I crave and enjoy the most.
When I eat out and ask for a salad I am always completely optimistic about what I may receive but almost always underwhelmed and dispassionate when it arrives. A few leaves, a ring of onion and a handful of cherry tomatoes covered in some kind of oil does not a salad make!

The salad is about to become your party piece. The crowning glory and centrepiece of every single meal including your best and most lavish dinner party.

I have hosted private dining events and the raw salad is the most dominant part of the menu, taking up half the table. Not only does it look impressive with all its colours and textures, it tastes divine and is always a big but pleasant shock to the diners. They have never seen or tasted salad quite like it.

Why do I refer to it as "raw"? Raw food retains 100% of its unaltered nutrients because it is still in its whole food, unprocessed state. As soon as we start to cook food, we are altering its structure, hence we begin to lose some of the nutrients. The more we cook or process foods, the less nutrition they will hold. Hence why the biggest part of your daily plate needs to be the raw salad.

We need fibre to keep a healthy gut. Nutrients cling to the fibre. The best way to introduce the fibre and nutrients to our bodies is to eat food in its purest form and to eat as many varieties and colours as we possibly can. This will give us the greatest chance of ingesting as wide an array of nutrients as possible, which the body can then process, distribute, and feed our nutrient hungry cells, satiating them for hours at a time.

This brings me nicely to a change that you will notice when your eating habits change. You will feel fuller for longer. You will snack less in-between meals. You will not feel the post food fatigue, aka the sugar slump, following eating.

The reason for this is very simple. It is because you are finally giving your body what it needs and wants. Nutrition.

When you get hungry, this is a signal from your body telling your brain that it is low on nutrients; it is saying "please go find some nutrients and top me up."

When you try to satisfy that need with processed foods, such as having a mid-morning cake or biscuit, maybe a sandwich, crisps, and a sugary drink at lunch time, or a bar of chocolate for the mid-afternoon pick me up, instead of topping up your nutrient levels, all you are doing is temporarily satisfying the craving. You put the nutrition-less food in the tank, the body is momentarily joyful as it feels food going in.

It sets to work breaking it down, pulling it apart looking for the nutrients that it needs to shoot through to the bloodstream. . . . But instead, all it finds are refined sugars, bad fats, lots of salt, and very little nutrition. Imagine its disappointment.

Because there is little to no nutrition in that food load, the body can't do anything with it so, it gets dispersed to the cells to be stored as fat, usually around the abdominal area, hence the 'spare tyre' phenomenon that occurs as we reach middle age. The cells are still nutrient hungry, so again it sends out signals to **"feed me."**

This is why you will find yourself sluggish while the body tries to deal with the empty nutrient but calorie-high food load and feel seemingly hungry again after only a short time.

Instead of reaching for the easy junk food for satiating these cravings, instead start to replace them with fruit and berries; make a smoothie blend to have throughout the day; or perhaps pre-prepare a big salad box crammed full of leaves and berries, nuts, seeds, grains, edible flowers; dress it up with a zingy **mango**, **chilli** and **lime** dressing; home-made of course! that you can then graze on, with zero guilt and maximum nutrition, all day long.

Your body will be singing happily as it processes and extracts and disperses those nutrients all around your body. It will be sated for hours and will ask for no more. You will feel full but light of body; your brain will be clear, your energy high, and you will emanate a glow that radiates from within.

For quick reference, I have listed foods for each of the categories as noted on our food heart on the following tables, beginning with our raw salad items:

RAW SALAD: 40% to 50% of Your Daily Plate

Herbs	Flowers	Grains	Beans and Legumes
Basil	Honeysuckle	Couscous	Chickpeas
Mint	Allium (Chive)	Quinoa	Lentils
Chives	Lovage	Millet	Butter Beans
Coriander	Dandelion	Wholegrain Brown Rice	Black Turtle
Parsley	Violet	Barley	Adzuki
Tarragon	Marigold	**Vegetables**	Broad
Dill	Pansies	Broccoli	Canellini
Oregano	Viola	Cabbage	Kidney
Marjoram	Nasturtiums	Cauliflower	Peas
Lemon Balm	Calendula	**Additional**	Pinto
Thyme	Chamomile	Avocado	Borlotti
Rosemary	Lavender	Seaweed flakes	Sweetcorn

Leafage	Salad Vegetables	Salad Fruits	Nuts and Seeds
Iceberg	Sugar Snap Peas	Apples	*See note re: soaking*
Rocket (Arugula)	Radishes	Oranges	Walnuts
Romaine	Cucumber	Pears	Pecans
Lambs Lettuce	Celery	Cherries	Pine
Watercress	Mushrooms	Blueberries	Brazil
Peashoots	Tomatoes	Blackberries	Pistachio
Spinach	**Raw Onions**	Tangerines	Cashew
Red Lettuce	White, Brown, Red	Raspberries	Sunflower
Radichio (Red Chicory)	Shallots	Kiwi	Pumpkin
Bok Choy	Spring	Pomegranate	Coriander
Endives	Fennel Bulb	Grapes	Mustard
Celery Tops	Celeriac	Mango	Chia
Fennel tops	Courgette/Marrow	Strawberries	Hemp
Nasturtium Leaves	Tomato Varieties	Pineapple	Sesame

Non-Starchy Vegetables, Greens, and Fruits: 30% to 40%

Gently **steaming** food is more efficient than boiling. This process helps to retain more intact nutrients in the food, whereas in boiling, much of the nutrients are lost and destroyed, thrown out with the water used to boil them in.

Steaming involves placing your vegetables and greens in a colander covered with a lid that sits above the water level in the pan underneath. Steam gently until the vegetables and greens are just starting to soften but still hold their shape and crunch, rather than turning to mush.

More nutrients will be kept in the food this way, especially by not overcooking them. I often drink the steam waters, particularly from spinach, so I can use up all those nutrients. It's also great to use as stock for oil free "frying," "roasting," or as a base for making sauces.

NON-STARCHY FOODS: 30% to 40% of Your Daily Plate

Vegetables	Mushrooms	Peppers	Citrus
Artichoke	Brown	Bell	Lemon
Asparagus	Button	Chilli	Lime
Aubergine	Chestnut	Jalapeno	Oranges
Broccoli	King Oyster	Fruits	Satsuma
Cabbage	Oyster	Apples	Tangerine
Cavalo Nero	Portobello	Apricots	Grapefruit
Celeriac	Shitake	Banana	**Berries**
Celery	**Onions**	Cherries	Blackberries
Courgette	Brown	Grapes	Blueberries
Chilli Peppers	Pickling	Kiwi	Gooseberries
Cauliflower	Shallots	Mango	Raspberries
Ginger	Spring	Melon	Strawberries
Green Beans	Red/White	Pears	
Other	Garlic	Pomegranate	
Kale	Kohlrabi	Plums	
Swiss Chard	Spinach		

As you can see, many of the ingredients listed can be incorporated into your salads, or included in smoothie blends.

These make for great lunches to take to work as they will keep you full without that heavy sluggish feeling as well as maintaining your energy levels throughout the day.

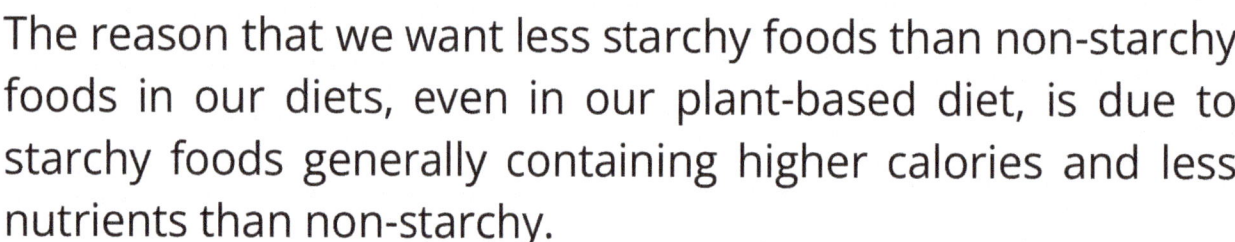

Steamed and Cooked Starchy Vegetables, Grains, Beans, and Fruits: Aim for 15% to 20%

The reason that we want less starchy foods than non-starchy foods in our diets, even in our plant-based diet, is due to starchy foods generally containing higher calories and less nutrients than non-starchy.

Think how you feel after eating a packed nutrient dense salad with your oil free dressing. You feel very full but your body still feels light and fresh. You feel satisfied, happy, energetic, and your taste buds are tingling with all the flavours and textures within that salad dish.

Now consider how you feel after consuming say the traditional British Sunday roast, and as we are on a meat/fish/dairy-free diet, swap out the meat element with a processed vegan-style meat, such as "no chicken" or "no turkey" alternatives for example.

The Sunday roast is typically very high in starchy foods that have been saturated in cooking oil; the vast amount of nutrients that were there, are lost during the cooking process. We have a meal that is high and heavy with calories but low in nutrients. We feel full, yes. But in an entirely different way to that full feeling after consuming the salad.

Now we are feeling heavy, sluggish, tired.. . . We may have to pop open that zipper or button on our jeans. We feel like we need a little sleep to "get over" the Sunday roast.

How many times have you seen your dad crash out after Sunday roast while mother is left to clean up the dishes!! I'm not being sexist here . . . it is what it is and it was no different in my childhood family home back through the 70s and 80s as it is today. Times may have changed but the effects of food and our human conditions have not!

Our body is working extra hard to process all those dense high calorie foods and in the end it reaps very little benefit. Like putting your all into a marathon, digging deep using up every bit of energy to get to that finish line, but just as it appears in sight, you trip up and fall flat on your face. All that effort for very little reward.

STARCHY FOODS: 15% to 20% of Your Daily Plate

Vegetables	Beans, Grains, Legumes, Pulses		
Butternut Squash	Adzuki Beans	Kidney Beans	Rice**
Carrots (cooked)	Borlotti Beans	Pinto Beans	Rye
Parsnips	Butter Beans	**Grains**	Spelt
Peas	Black Eyed Peas	Barley	**Fruit**
Potatoes	Black Turtle Beans	Couscous*	Dried
Red	Cannellini Beans	Millet	Figs
Sweet	Chickpeas	Oats	Plaintain (Banana)
White	Lentils (Red, Green)	Quinoa	Sultanas

*Couscous is considered to be more of a processed grain. It is made up of Durum Wheat or Semolina Flour.

**Wholegrain Rices only. The outer husk that is usually removed during heavy processing to produce the typical white rice most often consumed is where all the nutrients are retained.

DRY STORE and PANTRY

The dry store. This has been the absolute favourite change and addition to my kitchen. Where once "dry store" meant crisps, biscuits, and crackers for cheese, since moving to plant-based this has taken on a whole new meaning and image.

My dry store pantry did not happen along all at once. It has been built up over time, years in fact, and is still growing. I'm constantly adding, changing, and discovering new items as I go along. I get a huge amount of pleasure and satisfaction from sourcing new ingredients and learning how to use them to their best advantage.

Discoveries such as "Rose Harissa," a Lebanese flavour that adds a wonderfully fiery kick to any dish, more middle eastern flavours of "Za'ata'r" and "Dukkah" through to "Ras El Hanout" originating from North Africa all add interest, depth and flavour, as well as inspiring me to be more adventurous in my culinary creations.

There is no right or wrong way to build your dry store pantry. Do it gradually over time as you find your feet with your new way of eating and cooking. You'll discover so many new flavours, textures and varieties of foods and this will lead you to finding your own favoured and most needed dry store items.

To give you an idea of the kinds of items that you may find very useful, the chart over lists some items from my own dry store.

THE DRY STORE and PANTRY GUIDE

My Top Essentials	Herbs and Spices	Dry Goods: Grains	Dry/Tins in Water: Beans
Apple Cider Vinegar	Basil	Barley	Adzuki
Arrowroot Powder	Black Peppercorns	Couscous	Black Turtle
Ground Flaxseed	Cayenne	Green Lentils	Borlotti
Hulled Hempseed	Chipotle Flakes	Millet	Butter
Miso	Cinnamon	Oates	Cannellini
Nutritional Yeast Flakes	Coriander	Red Lentils	Chickpea (Garbanzo)
Seaweed Flakes	Crushed Chilli Flakes	**Flour:**	Pinto
Sodium Bicarbonate	Cumin	Almond	Red Kidney
Chia Seeds	Ginger	Buckwheat	**Other:**
Kala Namak	Garlic Powder	Coconut	Dates (Medjool)
Tahini	Italian Herbs	Gram (Chickpea)	Sultanas

Handy Bits and Bobs	Herbs and Spices	Flour:	Other:
Silicon Sheets	Onion Powder	Rye	Maple Syrup
Foil	Oregano	Spelt	Vanilla Ess
Measuring Spoons	Paprika	**Nuts and Seeds:**	Tahini
Digital Scales	Smoked Paprika	Brazil	Chia Seeds
Tea Strainers	Thyme	Cashew	Cacao Nibs
Ball of String	Turmeric	Pecan	*Cocoa
Sieves	White Pepper	Pine	*Maca
Jars	Nutmeg	Pistachio	*Matcha
Storage Containers	Dulse Seaweed Flakes	Walnuts	*Wheatgrass
Citrus Zester	Seaweed	Pumpkin	*Spirulina
Melon Baller for Avocado	Irish Moss Seaweed	Sunflower Seeds	Zuma Hot Chocolate

*These can all be bought in powder form.

Oils. There is no mention at all of any oils to cook or to make dips or dressings with. In a typical kitchen you would at least expect to find olive oil, coconut oil, or some kind of oily medium to make dressings, baste, fry, and roast with. Simply put, I don't use any!

A little note about oils

Consumption of refined oils in our diets through cooking methods or adding them to our foods is not, in my belief, good for our health. Dr. Joel Fuhrman recommends no more than a teaspoon of an oil, such as olive oil, PER DAY.

Oils are a by product, derived from processing the original whole food form; seeds, nuts and beans. It is mostly fat and calories. Any nutrition is thrown out, still clinging to the fibres of the whole food that it was extracted from.

Many oils that are deemed healthy are, in fact, still saturated fats, solid at room temperature; not healthy when eaten in daily quantities.

Similarly, when oils are heated to high temperatures for example when roasting or deep frying, particularly when the same oil is reheated numerous times, the high heat produces carcinogenic chemicals very dangerous to human health.

Ideally, we are looking to eat a balance of unsaturated and saturated fats that are still in their fibrous form.
What I mean by this is that they are still part of their original wholefood form. For example, instead of pouring avocado oil over our salad, eat the flesh from the whole, unprocessed avocado. The same applies to coconut, olives, and nut oils.

This way, we get all of the nutrients from the fibres rather than the fat and empty calories from the oil alone.

When I first began cooking wholly plant-based and cut out using oils for roasting, frying, basting, making sauces, and dressings, I found it tough! I was so used to covering everything in oil in the belief it was really good for me; it seemed alien not to use it.

Further, to sub oil out in place of water or stock was plain old crazy!

It took me a while to get the hang of this new way of cooking but, over time, I got better at it. Within a few months I could no longer stand the taste of oil; I hated (and still do) the film it would leave on my food and in my mouth. It really inhibits the flavour and texture of food, making everything greasy to taste and touch.

This includes all my kitchen appliances! I have a much cleaner kitchen now, without oils, than I did previously. Less cleaning is a definite bonus!

Take a deep dive into my recipe section that follows on in the second section of this book; you will see how easy it is to sub out oils in cooking and instead start using water or stock. This, too, is when your dry store will come in to play. Ingredients like miso, nutritional yeast flakes, and flax and hemp seeds will become the stars of your show as you slowly start to learn how to flavour and season naturally, to your own liking. Together with the myriad of herbs and spices that are readily available, you'll wonder why you ever needed oils in the first place.

Each and every single herb, spice, and natural flavouring that you use comes with its own powerhouse of nutrients that benefit every system of your body. From lowering blood pressure and reducing inflammation to promoting and enhancing your good gut bacteria and strengthening your immunity. You will become a font of knowledge as you discover the hundreds and even thousands of everyday and exotic herbs, spices, and flavourings there are.

I think you need to make some space in your kitchen; you're going to need it!

A few other common items missed off my dry store pantry include refined table, sea, and rock salts. Rather than using these refined versions, I now use miso paste to add a salt kick where needed.

Refined sugars also do not get a mention, for obvious reasons. We have a number of ways of sweetening dishes without resorting to the white stuff. There is no "in moderation" here for me. My advice: Omit! Omit! Omit!

Instead, opt for a small amount of maple syrup or make your own date syrup. This is super easy. Just add your dates to a pan with a bit of water and warm through until the dates have turned into a runny paste. You can also do the same with apples.

You will find that the more you transition and adapt to this new way of eating, the more developed and alive your taste buds will become.

Apples will be the sweetest, juiciest you've ever noticed and that fake sugar? It will be a "No thank you" as its taste will become too sickly sweet to stomach.

Bleached flours are a definite "off my list" too. I have listed out the flours I prefer to use (including easily making your own by simply milling down oats. I love sprouted whole grain oats as they are still full of nutrition having been soaked, sprouted and dried already). Because I now cook and eat differently, I have little use for even the "healthier alternative" flours as noted in the table, however we all love a sweet treat so they were definitely deserving of a place on the pantry list.

I'd really like to pay homage to my grandparents here. For it was my grandparents who inspired my love of cooking. Brought up in the countryside in the 70s, we grew most of our own food in our shared allotments across three houses that included two bountiful orchards of fruits and berries between us. My grandparents had spent their young adulthoods fighting a world war and suffering all the atrocities of loss and hardship that entailed.

I can only imagine their joy, and the joy of a nation, as rations slowly came to an end and suddenly all those sugars and fats and dairy denied them for so long made an appearance back at their tables. I do not decry this in any way; I likely would have been eating up every bit of apple pie with butter laden sugary crusts and large scoops of thick creamy milky custard myself!

They did not know then what we know now; how these foods can have a detrimental effect on us in so many ways.

It is well recorded too however, that those rationed years boasted the healthiest population the UK had seen.
Now that we know so much more about processed foods, we are much better placed to embrace a diet that once they had no choice in.

I hope that my dry store pantry and food tables are helpful to you. My advice is to print them out and pop them on your fridge, together with the good food and cheat food hearts.

Take the food tables shopping with you or make a smaller list choosing a few ingredients at a time.

Tick off those that you purchase and try marking off those you really like and scrubbing off those that you try but don't like. It won't take long to build your own personal dry store and pantry.

Because I am fast tracking you towards a plant-based diet, I have not gone into detail explaining each ingredient on my tables.

You can take a deep dive into this information, and much more, by joining my networking community.

Skip over to the next page to find out how!

'I'm not a Rabbit'

Strictly for very busy humans who want to eat more

Plant-based

but need help getting started and staying on course

Preparing your time

This one is a biggy.

When I talk to people about transitioning and what they find difficult, this is the reason most given: "I don't have time."

We all have our daily and weekly routines, driven by all the factors that make up our days and weeks at various stages of our lives; work commitments, parenting, family responsibilities, domestic duties, social commitments. We do need structure in our lives because we are all so busy and when we are faced with a big change, such as changing how we eat, it can be very daunting just thinking about where and how that change will fit into everything else you already undertake. Preparing your time is interconnected with the mindset change; it is still a change that needs to begin with a change of mind.

There is no way around this; if you want to eat differently you will have to make a few changes here and there with your time so that you **can** implement new routines. And that's all this is; it's forming a new daily/weekly/monthly routine.

Instead of viewing this in a negative light, look at this with positivity. This is a change that will impact your life positively. It will add joy because you will have better health, less sickness, more energy, better skin, a clearer mind.

You will feel much more in control of your life; you are purposefully choosing what to put in your body and you are making time to allow that to happen.

A couple of years ago, I was given a beautiful book by my good friend Derek. I loved how he presented it to me. . . . He had wrapped it up in brown parcel paper, tied together with string. The book is called **Hygge**.

I felt the full meaning of this word as soon as the book was presented to me; it was given with the intention of making me happy, passing me a piece of joy that Derek had experienced when he was first given the book.

Hygge, pronounced "Whoo-girr" is a Danish word that means "the art of happiness."

What has this got to do with anything that we are talking about right now? Everything!

Hygge is not just a word; it's a practice. The Danish have perfected this. You can use this practice yourself to help you embrace the changes you are making right now, not just your food changes, any changes. Hygge means something different to everyone. For me, things that I consider to be my Hygge would be:

Dancing in my kitchen with friends on cocktail nights, they fill my home with love, laughter, and happiness as we forget all our worries and enjoy that moment of togetherness.

Hugging my grandson, knowing how blessed I am to have him in my life; there is no better hug to be had.

Cooking. The act of immersing myself in the process of creating a recipe from a simple thought, then buying or foraging for whatever ingredients are needed. I allow myself time so I can turn up my favourite **music** while I get lost in the preparation of food for the day, or even the week ahead.

I don't notice the hours go by as my kitchen fills with wonderful aromas and I get the joy of seeing food being prepared, knowing those hours have just saved me time while I'm busy with work and all the other myriad of "things" that make up my week. I know I will eat well no matter how busy or tired I am during my work week.

Writing this book. Being so busy myself, I knew that it would be tough to find time to complete this. Instead of getting stressed about it, I made it a time of Hygge. Working with my diary I would jot down slots of time each week that I knew I could use for writing. They became my moments of joy instead of moments of frustration, "I need to get this done but I haven't got time" or "I'll never get this done."

If you see the changes as something positive, they do become joyful experiences.

Everyone has a different schedule; our lives are all different, there is no "one size fits all" here with how you will embrace and use your time differently. To help you, I will tell you how I approached it for myself.

I started to keep a daily diary. I like an actual diary, like the old-fashioned way of time keeping. But I do know that lots of people like to keep a diary on their phones. Whichever way works for you, I encourage you to keep a diary. I use mine very simply. I note down every appointment I have for each day. For example a typical Monday for me is 8am to 4pm office based work, 6.30pm a fitness session.

Because that is pretty much set in stone as a routine, I can write that up in my diary for a few weeks ahead. Already I know on a Monday I have some time between 4pm and 6.30pm that I can use for say, shopping for ingredients or writing my book, creating content for my website, etc.

Every day is the same; there are certain things I know I will be doing at specific times. So I write these up a few weeks ahead then I look to see what gaps of time I have to do other things.

By doing this, I realised that Sunday was my best day for cooking. It's easier for me to cook in bulk for the week ahead because the most time I have is on a Sunday. So that's what I do.

This has become a Hygge time for me. I look forward to it. It's my time; I am the queen of my kitchen and not even the cat bothers me. She knows too! I make it special by putting my favourite playlists on Spotify, turning it up, and singing and dancing along as I cook.

I love the process of getting all my utensils out that I'll use; preparing the food and weighing out everything I need. Once this prep is done, I cook. It's become my routine and I'm so well versed in it that I don't think about it. It's become a new routine so much so that what used to take me say five hours now takes me half the time.

Spending four hours on a Sunday cooking may not work for you. Your time may work better in smaller increments on different days. If you have children it's great to get them involved too so you can all share the experience together. This will also help your children begin to form good habits and create their Hygge moments for themselves.

I have the happiest memories of spending time with my grandmother as she cooked and baked her way through her days. That was our Hygge. Neither of us knew the word or practice back then but now I look back, I realise how loving and joyful those times were. I was with the person I loved and adored most in the world; at the same time I was learning from her. My own children used to love being in the kitchen with me; food time was family time. My son is now a professional chef and has worked in kitchens from michelin star to country restaurant. I know his great grandmother will be beaming with love and pride, knowing that something she shared with me has been passed down the generations and has resulted in her great grandson taking it to the highest professional level.

Identify the gaps of times that you have in your daily and weekly life; use this knowledge to then start to change how you shop for food and then cook. You might find cooking every day works best for you or maybe, like me, one day a week works better.

Whatever works best for you is key

Be patient with yourself. This is new and the change will not happen all at once. Rather it's a transition. It will take some time to adjust but, enjoy the process.

At one time, my diet was pretty much eating whatever was the quickest, and most convenient, with no real regard to how my food choices could affect my physique or health.

Then, my mindset started to change. I didn't feel good. I was nearing middle age and already I could see that if I continued on the same path, I would become ill as well as continue to gain pounds on top of pounds. It felt miserable. I knew I needed to change. I retreated into a chrysalis state, spending my time researching and reading, watching medical documentaries, following plant-based doctors and physicians, studying to whatever level I could that would give me more knowledge to help myself on this journey. And eventually I emerged again. Into the new me, the butterfly version.

You don't need to go through all of those phases that I did. This was my reason for writing this book. I have too strong an urge to share what I've learnt so that you and everyone one around you can benefit now. Not in five years or ten years time, but today.

The food heart was created very much on the back of me reading lots of books written by plant-based doctors, physicians and healthcare professionals, that I have discovered and followed over the years.

I have recommended, or passed on, many of the books I've read myself, to both friends and guests who attended my workshops or events, with the intention that the readings may make their own transitions easier.

The gesture is always received well, but often I'm told that the medical style writing is a bit off-putting, making the read less enjoyable or engaging and it was still not clear **how** to include plant-based eating into everyday life.

The solution to help make it easier was a 'doodling accident' !

I was idly sketching away on a piece of scrap paper at my desk job (sorry boss!!) one day, drawing hearts. I started to add in pictures of food, similar to the more traditional food pyramid and after a few minutes I had in front of me a simple visual aid that was nice to look at and easy to understand.
The **food heart** was born!

Tom, my son, then suggested the '**cheat food heart**' which is included later on in the book (see page 81).

The food hearts gave me the starting point for writing this book, which is now the guide and "instructions" on how to use the food hearts for everyday eating.

I have thoroughly enjoyed writing these pages. It has been a challenge for sure but, I have felt very supported by my wonderful, caring family and friends who have listened to me endlessly talking about content, recipes, food hearts, nutrition, platforms, and apps for months! Their patience and love is boundless; I am blessed to be surrounded, supported, and loved by such beautiful people.

As you've read through the pages, I truly hope you have felt loved, supported, listened to, and understood by me. And I hope that I have been able to succeed in getting you started on the path to better eating habits, loving food, loving life, and making great changes for a healthier, happier, and longer future.

Part 3
The Shopping Guide

Shopping for plant-based foods

It can be tricky knowing what to buy when you're trying to eat healthier, and eating plant-based can be even trickier. So, to give you a head start and some practical guidance, I've included a table for each of the different categories from the food heart.

Let's make a start with my favourite, salads.

I like to build my salads using whatever fresh raw ingredients that are seasonally available, starting with items like green apples, sugar snap peas, radishes, broccoli florets, celery, cucumber, shredded celeriac or fennel bulb, sliced raw onions, scallions (spring onions), and tomatoes, and then start adding in some starches, such as a handful of peas, maybe some steamed carrot or butternut squash, or a couple of tablespoons of chickpeas.

Then I like to add a splash of apple cider vinegar and/or balsamic vinegar with some seasonings, anything that floats my boat that day. Handfuls of various leaves, shredded iceberg, rocket, lambs lettuce, watercress, peashoots, endives, microgreens in handfuls, and fresh aromatic herbs such as coriander, basil, and mint make a fab addition to the flavours here. Berries, nasturium leaves, and flowers are probably my favourite salad items that I can pick from my own garden.

Nasturtium leaves are very peppery and the flowers have a deep but delicate flavour to them and add a wonderful vibrant fiery splash of colour to the bowl. The end result becomes a work of art, worthy of a place in anyone's digital photo album.

Versatile, inventive.

Be inventive and be you!

Salads are versatile, delicious, and totally up to what you like and how you like it.

So don't be afraid to experiment with new ingredients; buy a small amount first to see if you like it. Use different herbs and add spices for additional flavourings.

Oil free dressings are surprisingly easy to make yet super healthy.

My favourite oil free dressing **"mango, chilli and lime"** really adds a huge flavour kick when drizzled over the top of my monumental salads. I've included a quick recipe for that in the recipe book that accompanies this guide. See 'Section 05 - Oil Free Dressings and Pesto' if you want to jump straight in and make this gorgeous, zingy dressing.

I would love to see your salad creations, so please, take lots of pics and video's! You can send them in to me at my site;

www.benourished.im

I'm always looking for new idea's and would happily feature your own salad as a special on my website, to inspire others as well as myself.

Examples of RAW SALAD: 40% to 50% of Your Daily Plate

Herbs	Flowers	Grains	Beans and Legumes
Basil	Honeysuckle	Couscous	Chickpeas
Mint	Allium (Chive)	Quinoa	Lentils
Chives	Lovage	Millet	Butter Beans
Coriander	Dandelion	Wholegrain Brown Rice	Black Turtle
Parsley	Violet	Barley	Adzuki
Tarragon	Marigold	**Vegetables**	Broad
Dill	Pansies	Brocolli	Canellini
Oregano	Viola	Cabbage	Kidney
Marjoram	Nasturtiums	Cauliflour	Peas
Lemon Balm	Calendula	**Additional**	Pinto
Thyme	Chamomile	Avocado	Borlotti
Rosemary	Lavender	Seaweed Flakes	Sweetcorn

Leafage	Salad Vegetables	Salad Fruits	Toasted Nuts and Seeds
Iceberg	Sugar Snap Peas	Apples	*See note re: soaking*
Rocket (Arugula)	Radishes	Oranges	Walnuts
Romaine	Cucumber	Pears	Pecans
Lambs Lettuce	Celery	Cherries	Pine
Watercress	Mushrooms	Blueberries	Brazil
Peashoots	Tomatoes	Blackberries	Pistachio
Spinach	**Raw Onions**	Tangerines	Cashew
Red Lettuce	White, Brown, Red	Raspberries	Sunflower
Radichio	Shallots	Kiwi	Pumpkin
Bok Choy	Spring	Pomegranate	Coriander
Endives	Fennel Bulb	Grapes	Mustard
Celery Tops	Celeriac	Mango	Chia
Fennel Tops	Courgette	Strawberries	Hemp
Nasturtiums	Tomato Varieties	Pineapple	Sesame

As you can see from the table, it's very easy to make up your raw salad daily. I have only noted a mere few ingredients that spring to my mind; mostly those that are my go-to, favourite ingredients and the most readily available at my local stores, independent growers, and farmers markets. I could have continued writing that list for hours!

It's also very easy to include every other category of ingredients from our food heart within the salad itself. Sometimes this is just perfect for a hot summers day when you don't want or need anything more, except for maybe a nice, icy cold green gazpacho soup on the side. Perfect too as a filling and nutrient dense lunch to take to work. There'd be no 3 p.m. sugar slump after a huge bowl of that!

The salad, fruit, and vegetable aisles are usually the first aisles that you come to in your local supermarket. Make this your place to be; stop and really look at the array of ingredients that are on display. Don't be afraid to add something new to your list each time you shop.

Experimenting is great; I've discovered so many new greens, fruits and vegetables since becoming plant-based. Things I had either never heard of before, likely just walking past them as I headed for the familiar, or things I had seen but didn't know what to do with.

It's also a great way to discover new flavours, textures, and even methods of cooking.

The beauty of this part of our food heart plate is that, while most things are now available all year round, there is still plenty to offer to create a warm autumnal or winter salad too.

Every season offers us something new and exciting, helping us hit our nutrients whatever the time of year.

NON STARCHY FOODS: 30% to 40% of Your Daily Plate

Vegetables	Mushrooms	Peppers	Citrus
Artichoke	Brown	Bell	Lemon
Asparagus	Button	Chilli	Lime
Aubergine	Chestnut	Jalapeno	Oranges
Broccoli	King Oyster	**Fruits**	Satsuma
Cabbage	Oyster	Apples	Tangerine
Cavalo Nero	Portobello	Apricots	Grapefruit
Celeriac	Shitake	Banana	**Berries**
Celery	**Onions**	Cherries	Blackberries
Courgette	Brown	Grapes	Blueberries
Chilli Peppers	Pickling	Kiwi	Gooseberries
Cauliflower	Shallots	Mango	Raspberries
Ginger	Spring	Melon	Strawberries
Green Beans	Red	Pears	
Garlic	White	Pomegranate	
Kohlrabi	Kale	Plums	
Spinach	Sprouts	Swiss Chard	

STARCHY FOODS: 15% to 20% of Your Daily Plate

Vegetables	Beans, Grains, Legumes, Pulses	Beans, Grains, Legumes, Pulses	Beans, Grains, Legumes, Pulses
Butternut Squash	Adzuki Beans	Kidney Beans	Rice**
Carrots (cooked)	Borlotti Beans	Pinto Beans	Rye
Parsnips	Butter Beans	**Grains**	Spelt
Peas	Black Eyed Peas	Barley	**Fruit**
Potatoes	Black Turtle Beans	Couscous*	Dried
Red	Cannellini Beans	Millet	Figs
Sweet	Chickpeas	Oats	Plaintain (Banana)
White	Lentils (Red, Green)	Quinoa	Sultanas

*Couscous is considered to be more of a processed grain. It is made up of Durum Wheat or Semolina Flour.

**Wholegrain Rices only. The outer husk that is usually removed during heavy processing to produce the typical white rice most often consumed is where all the nutrients are retained.

Nutritional Yeast Flakes

Vitamin B12 is well-known to be deficient in a predominantly plant-based diet; however, I know more people who include meat, fish, and dairy in their diets to be deficient of this vitamin than those who follow the predominantly plant-based or vegan diet. This may be due to more awareness that we need to supplement up on this vitamin if we choose to eradicate meat, fish, and dairy from our diets. Adding nutritional yeast flakes to your daily diet is a great way to get more of the B complex vitamins in your system.

Ground Flaxseed

As well as a host of beneficial nutrients, ground flaxseed also contains one of the two essential fatty acids required in your daily diet for heart health: ALA, which is a type of omega 3.

Adding a tablespoon of each over your salads, in your smoothies, or on your hot dishes is a fantastic and easy way to include all the benefits that these two superfoods offer. Happily, I can tell you that these items can easily be purchased in your local Supermarket and Health Food stores. These are now on the shelves as everyday products, which is so good to see. The big supermarkets are hearing our cries for healthier options and are slowly starting to respond.

Seaweed Flakes

Seaweed flakes, such as "Nori" or "dulse," are used to add essential iodine and an impressive array of other nutrients to your daily diet. I use a teaspoon of Nori or dulse seaweed flakes in my oil-free pesto and in many other recipes, including two of my favourites: my plant-based no tuna mayo mix that's made with chickpeas instead of tuna and my plant-based chowder.

Chia Seeds

Did you know that chia seeds are part of the mint family? They are the edible seeds of a flowering plant that is native to southern Mexico.

They have many noted health benefits including gut health and digestion. Add a tablespoon to your smoothies and fruit bowls, or make a delicious overnight chia seed cocoa pudding ready for a super nutritious breakfast.

Just as a footnote here; it is possible now to purchase items such as ground flaxseed, nutritional yeast, and seaweed flakes in your local supermarkets and health food stores, so you don't have to worry about trying to source these ingredients from specialist or niche stores anymore.

Kitchen Gadgets

The following kitchen gadgets are my essentials that help me by making food/meal preparation quicker and more efficient, saving me time when I'm at my busiest but I still want to eat healthily.

Food Blender

This is by far my most used, loved, and essential piece of kit in the kitchen. Its uses are so versatile and varied. I make smoothies in it, sauces, salad dressings, desserts, healthy cake mixes. I simply could not live, or rather cook, without it.

Mine is a 1000w digital hands-free Ninja. It's powerful and I can throw my ingredients in, press the button, and leave it be to work its magic while I get on with other things.

Ninjas are widely available in your local Currys or Dixons stores, online on Amazon, or you can use Facebook Marketplace and buy one second hand for a lot less money. I've had a few over the years but they seem to go on forever. All I've had to do is buy new blades.

They are neat and look great on the kitchen countertop, taking up little space. I have two out on my worktop. They never get put away because I use them every day.

New Ninja Blenders start at around £50 for a 700w and increase to around £200 for a 1000w with more attachments.

Small Ingredient Chopper

This is my second most used and essential (Ninja) gadget. It saves so much time! No more crying over chopping your raw onions or struggling with that pesky garlic.

A quick peel and rough chop of your onions is all that's needed, then you can throw them in the chopper, pop the lid on, press it down, and voila! You have chopped onions in seconds. The same with garlic. I cut the end of my garlic cloves, then press the flat of the knife over the clove and bash it with the heel of my hand. This releases the skin very effectively and quickly.

Pop them in the chopper and you have chopped garlic.

Its perfect for making risotto base, which is typically onion, garlic, and celery. Everything can be rough chopped, popped in, and a few seconds later you have your finely chopped base ready to put in the pan.

Tip: I sub out white arborio rice and replace it with the healthier alternative of barley or "riced cauliflower" for my risottos.

Oil free pestos are a breeze when made in the chopper. The blades are very sharp (so be careful) and powerful and the drum is just the right size for making pesto (see recipe section on how to make this without oil or parmesan)

They cost around £30 and come with two barrels and lids for handy storage in the fridge. They are small so they don't take up much space in the kitchen, are easy to clean, and last a long time. I've had mine for years and it's as good now as it was when I first bought it.

A good set of kitchen knives

Good knives are a great investment. These can be bought individually, one at a time, to save you having to pay lots all at once.

A decent knife set will save you a lot of time as they slice cleanly and make the job a lot easier. Choose your own set of knives to suit you; it's a very personal thing.

My go to are steel mid weight with good grip/anti-slip handles, although over the years I've had so many different types.

My favourite knife was gifted to me by a friend, a Damascus complete with a sharpener and a lovely case to store it in.

A set of chopping boards

I love my coloured chopping boards and use the different colours for different foods. One colour is dedicated for strong aroma foods like garlic, onions, etc., another colour is for fruits and berries, another for mushrooms, and so on. This also helps with cross contamination.

Another way of keeping dedicated boards for different food types is to get your board "branded." An artist or engraver will be able to do this by "burning" letters into it. This is more expensive but it does look really smart and can make a fab gift.

Air Fryer

Quite possibly the best invention this century! My best purchase has been this wonderful gadget that makes cooking without oils and fats easy.

Instead of using oils to cook and crisp up foods, the air fryer uses hot air. It's unreal how effective this is. Some benefits of cooking this way:

- Healthier—no oil needed. I sometimes put a little water in the tray, never oil
- It's super quick; much quicker than a conventional oven
- Easy to clean
- Small enough to fit on the kitchen countertop

- Crispy food in no time
- Cooks evenly and quickly, retaining moisture
- Suitable for most foods as long as they are not covered in wet batter

There are so many different models out now and as ever Ninja have hit the nail on the head with their version. The Ninja Foodi Max Dual version has two separate tray compartments so you can simultaneously cook different foods at different temperatures for varying lengths of time and have everything ready at the same time.

Aside from Ninja there are many different styles and versions to choose from to suit your needs and budget. Tower does a very good air fryer, priced at around the £50 to £60 mark; prices then rise up into the £100s depending on what your needs are. The most expensive I have seen retails at £250 for a Cusinart dual toaster 1800 watt Air Fryer Oven.

The downside of the air fryer at the time of writing this article is that for a family of four you would be unlikely to be able to cook an entire meal for the whole family and have it all ready and warm at the same time.

However, the good news is you can still use your conventional oven in the same way as an air fryer by cooking your roasts without using any oil. Oils and fats are instead replaced with water or stock.

I have been cooking this way for several years now and what I have found is that I now dislike foods cooked in fats. All I can taste is the coating of oil over the food and not the food itself. As you will see from my recipes that accompany this book, even my salad dressings omit oil. And I know you will love them as much as I do.

I would love to see commercial fryers replaced with commercial air fryers instead. How healthy would that be, not to mention the wider positive impact this would have on our environment. Where do all those waste rancid oils and fats go once they can't be used anymore? And where do they come from in the first place? A discussion for another book in the future!

Food Processor

This really is a handy piece of kit for the kitchen because, if like me, you are pushed for time, the food processor enables you to make up larger batches that can then be wrapped and stored in the freezer ready for those busy days when you don't have the time (or energy) to cook.

One of my favourite recipes that is made entirely in the food processor is my "Chickpea, Lime, and Coriander Burgers." I bulk make the mix up, shape the burgers, then wrap them individually in grease-proof paper, pop them in freezer bags or containers, and store them in the freezer, ready to whip out at a moments notice.

The burgers, or patties, whatever your preferred name for them is, do freeze well and can be cooked from frozen, straight from the freezer into the oven, still maintaining their flavour, colour and texture.

There is a wide range of food processors on the market; so finding one that suits your needs and budget will be easy.

The cheapest I've seen is a model made by Logik at £40; however Ninja wins out with their super duper 800 watt 2 litre capacity model coming in at £185.

Freezer friendly containers

Save those take away containers while you're still buying take aways; because after reading this book, they will become an occasional now and then treat rather than the traditional saturday night take away!!! Now we can prevent the need for landfills and put these to good use.

Every time I make anything I make sure I bulk up; I then put half into portion sized containers straight into the freezer. It soon builds up, before you know it you have your very own frozen food department in your own kitchen made without any of the preservatives and additives that are in many of the mass produced supermarket freezer goods.

Kilner/Glass Storage Jars

You are about to have a whole new pantry full of interesting, colourful dry store goods. This means you're going to need glass jars to store everything in, to keep them fresh and airtight for months, even years. I wash every jar out after I've used its contents, using nontoxic/plant-based washing up liquid. Once it's clean, I then pop it in the oven to give it a final sterilisation.

Kilner Jars are fab too; they look so pretty on the shelves in the kitchen. I even use them as vases and for filling with tiny fairy lights (they look fab dotted around the garden on a summer's night when you're having friends around).

I like to put labels on mine so I can record the contents and date; you will forget if you don't do this, trust me! Instead of using sellotape I like to tie the label on with pieces of string. When giving as gifts it's also lovely to tie in a small bunch of fragrant herbs or flowers. We all have jars so this is a great way to reuse them for years to come.

Silicon or grease-proof paper

Since omitting oils/fats from my diet, silicon paper has become a necessity. I use it to line baking trays and tins with instead of using oil. Check out my website 'benourished.im' and look for my recipe for no oil celeriac chips. They are steamed first, coated in spices and then baked in the oven on trays lined with silicon sheets. And yes, they do crisp up and stay fluffy in the middle! One hundred sheets cost around £10, are double sided, and be used four to five times. My local Jacs store stocks them and they can be found online easily too.

Part 4
Final Words

We are nearing the end of our time together within the confines of these pages. Thank you, from the bottom of my heart for your support and time to this point. I'm happy that you stayed the journey till near its end; it's greatly appreciated. Already I am planning a follow-up book having enjoyed this process so much.

I will finish by presenting you with the final piece of the Food Heart Method.
The "Cheat Food Heart"

This is just as important as the food heart itself. While the food heart tells you what you SHOULD eat, the cheat food heart tells you what you should eat in **moderation**, if at all

If we base our eating on the rule of 80% plant-based, then the cheat food heart represents the foods you need to avoid or at least refrain from eating, at the very most, 20% of the time. For those moments when you can't avoid or just fancy a "treat," then you know that you've got a 20% leeway. If you are eating 80% plant-based for nutrition, then your body will be much better able to cope with the smaller amounts of foods that aren't so good for you.

You will find, over time, in fact quite quickly, that your tastebuds come back to life. All the refined, sugary, highly salted foods we consume dumb this down and we lose a big part of our sense of taste. You will notice just how sweet an apple is or, conversely, just how salty that microwave meal tastes.

Put the food heart and the cheat food heart side by side, somewhere where you will see them on a daily basis. When I showed my daughter the food hearts, she looked up at me with a giggle "Mum, your cheat food heart is my actual diet." Like so many others, she eats the food hearts the opposite way around. Knowing that this method has helped her has really endorsed my belief that I am doing the right thing.

If you are the only person that I help, then writing this book and creating those food hearts has been worth doing. I hope to help thousands, in as many corners of the globe as possible. If you have found this book and the food hearts helpful, then please do tell as many people as you can. Share this with them so that they too can reap the benefits and take control of their lives and eating habits. Eating for nutrition is easy when you know how.

I promised you some recipes to help you get started. Before this, take a glance on the following page; here you will find your cheat food heart. Print that out and put it next to your food heart. They are about to become your food bibles.

Then its time to close this book and jump straight into the recipe book that follows directly after my recommendations list. These recipes will help to get you started with a few easy meal ideas.

If you want to add more recipes to your collection, head on over to find these, and more, on my website benourished.im.
I look forward to connecting with you there.

With love, gratitude and fabulous food

Michelle

Gratitude

It takes one person to write a book, but it takes a team to create a book that is worth reading. The following three people I owe the biggest gratitude to as, without them, my book would never have gotten any further than the manuscript it was first written on. Thank you Jon, Thomas, and Jan for guiding and helping me to get this out there. I could not have done this without you.

Jon, Studio Cooper A very big thank you from me to you. You turned my food hearts, from my scrappy pencil drawings and the thoughts in my head, into the food hearts that are displayed throughout this book and across my social media platforms. All of the graphics found in this book that relate to food hearts are Jon's creations, taking the information I gave him with the outcome I envisaged, only 1,000 times better than I ever imagined. A truly good gem of a find in graphic design.

Thomas, TN Media At one time, my writings were a simple word document. A straight, same font, one colour, same size, 73-page A4 manuscript of words. Thomas took this manuscript and transformed it into the book you've just read. He brought it alive with clever use of different fonts, colours, and positioning of paragraphs, headings and words in a way I could never have done myself. Thank you, Thomas, for breathing the life and vibrancy into this book and styling it so that every reader is kept interested and engaged throughout.

Jan Tinsley, Business Mentor What is a book without an audience? A dusty manuscript! So much gratitude to you Jan, for your unwavering support and belief in me. Your guidance, advice and on-going mentorship is invaluable. Without you keeping me accountable, helping me navigate through this process, my book would have remained a dream in my head.

I could not leave without also saying big thanks to:

KBS My fab friend Peter Radcliffe, KBS. Love, gratitude and more thanks than you can ever dream of go to you for your undying support throughout the many trials and tribulations of our long-standing friendship and kinship. As much as we infuriate each other (STFU!) we certainly inspire each other and when I have been down you have held out your hand to pick me up and for your love, kindness and unending belief and support of me, I can simply never find enough words to thank you.

Thom and Baba G: My comrades. Son and Fur baby. Thanks for all the cuddles and the late-night chats and . . . let's not forget Thom, that cheat food heart. As I showed you design #752 of food heart you said "Yeah, looks good motherrrr. What would be good too would be a food heart that shows all the stuff that's not so good for you." Voila! The cheat food heart was created and born that very night. Thank you, my love, for putting up with my never-ending ideas and constant babble about apps and hacks and eating habits and for giving me your ever balanced and well thought views as I progressed through this journey. Together with our cat, we make a very happy team.

Babs my "brain storm" pal. Thanks for listening, supporting, encouraging, meeting up, and throwing ideas around the table. You always inspire and motivate me. Even when I'm feeling stuck, you lift me and tell me to go get it done!!

Jo The wisest of them all. My lovely friend, where would I be and, who would I be, without you in my life, shining your constant light. I know no other person less judgemental and more loving, caring, and giving than you. I am blessed to have you as my friend. Thank you for always listening, encouraging, supporting, and debating with me on anything and everything that life can throw at us. I am stronger and more whole with you.

Amanda For your "eagle eyed" proofreading! You cannot know how invaluable it is to have that second set of eyes, scrutinising every letter over 150 pages of words. The final finishing touch that enabled this book to be released.

Jenn and the PYP team Jenn T. Grace, Alexander, Lily and the rest of the PYP team have been simply amazing to work with.

KISS! being my first book both written and then published, it has been a journey into the unknown for me. Throughout the process, the team have been patient, hand holding where needed, practical, empathetic as well as professional, wanting my book to be the best version that it could be.

Thank you guys, I appreciate you so much.

To YOU, dear reader

While we may not know each other in the physical, it is **YOU** who has been my drive and inspiration to write this book and create the **Food Heart Method**.
I truly wish you the happiest journey on this path of life through which we are all meandering.
May you embrace every day in good health, bright spirits, and bathe in the love of great friends, family, and the best foods that mother nature can give.
To your best health, always.

RECOMMENDATIONS

DOCUMENTARIES
Forks Over Knives
What The Health
That Vitamin Movie
Fat, Sick, and Nearly Dead
Hope
The Game Changers

BOOKS
Dr. Joel Fuhrman:
Eat To Live
Super Immunity
Fast Food Genocide
Dr. Michael Greger:
How Not To Die
How Not To Diet
How to Survive a Pandemic
T. Colin Campbell PhD:
The China Study
Whole
The Low Carb Fraud

MAGAZINES (Digital and Physical)
Vegan Food and Living
Plant Based News
VegNews
The Vegan Magazine
Plant Based Magazine

RECOMMENDATIONS

OTHER BOOKS:
Hygge: The Danish Art of Happiness
John Yudkin: Pure, White, and Deadly
Veg Every Day and Much More Veg: River Cottage
Ultra: Rich Roll
Gabrielle Bernstein: Super Attractor
Susan Jeffers: Feel The Fear and Do It Anyway

ONLINE RESOURCES:
Dr. Shireem Kassam (LinkedIn)
The Real Truth About Health Series (Youtube)
Nutritionfacts.org
Drfuhrman.com
PCRM.Org

PODCASTS:
Zoe: Food Science and Nutrition
In a Nutshell
The Simply Vegan Podcast
The Rich Roll Podcast
The Positive Mindset Podcast
Plantstrong
The Mindset Mentor
Feel Better, Live Longer with Dr. Ranjeen Chatterjee
Get Sleepy: Sleep Meditation and Stories
Calm It Down
Sleepy

Good Food

- raw salad
- non-starchy veg & greens
- starchy veg grains & beans
- berries & fruits
- healthy fats flaxseed
- nuts & seeds

80% daily

Cheat Food

- breads & pasta
- refined sugars
- dairy & eggs
- meat crisps fish
- sweets & candy
- bad fats

20% daily

'I'm not a Rabbit'

Strictly for very busy humans who want to eat more

Plant-based

but need help getting started and staying on course

KISS!
PLANT-BASED KICK STARTER RECIPES

Contents

01 Introduction

02 Breakfast: smoothies & muffins

03 All day bites & mains

04 Be nourished plate

05 Oil free dressings & pesto

06 Let's get starchy

07 Not so naughty sweetie

01 Introduction

I'm really excited to share the following recipes with you! These are typical dishes that I cook up for myself everyday at home, constructed in such a way so as to cover all my nutrient, fibre, and protein needs.

Many of the recipes that I create are, at some point or another, also sold in my home town on the beautiful Isle of Man, or used at food events and festivals that I attend both at home and around the UK.

Nothing on these pages will phase you at all. Even if you aren't a confident or enthusiastic cook, you will easily be able to put these dishes together.

Cooking is intuitive. A recipe is just a guide. You don't have to rigidly stick to the exact ingredients or even amounts.

Every recipe can, and should be, tweaked to your own liking.

Use this book as a handy guide, learning how to put nutrients on your plate instead of the traditional calorie counting and restrictive eating that is most common in our modern life.

Once you've made a recipe or two, you will find your confidence grow and fear dissipate. Soon, you'll be throwing together a range of different ingredients and creating your own super simple high nutrient dishes without a seconds thought.

Neither do these recipes take hours to make. I have deliberately kept the recipes simple and suitable for everyday cooking so you don't have to worry about trying to find long lists of ingredients or spending all night in the kitchen struggling to follow the instructions. There'll still be time for whatever hobbies or social time you engage in once the work day is done!

If you have already read the first section of this book ***KISS! Plant-Based Eating*** then you will recall my section on **Hygge.** Make these kitchen sessions something you look forward to and enjoy the process as your relationship with food changes and grows.

02 Breakfast: Smoothies and Muffins

BREAKFAST

Breakfast notes

I'm an early riser (not good at communicating till around 11am!) and I like to make sure that I get some good nutrition in my body to start my day well.

I love the three recipes that are to follow because all of these are actually super easy. Two of them take less than ten minutes, and all of them can be made in bulk and refrigerated for up to five days or, they can also be frozen and kept for several months.

This is where my "over cooking" comes in.

Whenever I cook anything, I always make too much, on purpose.

I use at least a third of the dish to consume that day and perhaps over the next two to three days; the rest I put into freezer friendly containers.

A good tip is to use the smaller containers that hold around 350 ml to 500 ml for things like smoothies. This means that you can defrost individual amounts at a time instead of taking out a whole litre of food that you can't eat all at once.

When freezing items such as lentil flatbreads or the super berry muffins, another tip is to wrap each individual flatbread or muffin in cellophane and then wrap again in foil. Pop them all into a freezer bag and they will freeze beautifully without the possibility of ice crystals getting in.

Breakfast notes

The main objective of eating plant-based is to eat as much nutrition as you possibly can. When you are making say, a smoothie, just think of how many additional nutrients you can add such as **microgreens**, **nuts**, **seeds**, **vegetables**, **fruits**, or **berries**. My breakfast recommendation is a warm muffin plus a smoothie to see you through till lunchtime.

You will have noted on the muffins recipe I mentioned making your own oat flour.

I highly recommend doing this rather than using bleached refined flour that has been sitting on a shelf for months and longer. The word "refined" makes it sound high end; however, it really means highly and unfavourably processed.

Ultimately, it belongs on the cheat food heart as an avoid or a bare minimum and certainly no more than 20% item.

Blueberry Muffin Smoothie

Breakfast. Snack. Pre and Post workout. In fact, just enjoy anytime!
Food Heart: Berries. Fruits. Raw. Starchy.

Ingredients

- 100g blueberries, fresh or frozen
- 1 ripe banana
- 180g oates
- Cinnamon, ground
- Maple syrup (opt)
- 1 litre non dairy milk
- ice cubes

Utensils

- Blender

Instructions

Throw all ingredients into your blender and blitz till smooth and creamy.

Decant into a glass or bowl, add a selection of fresh blueberries, nuts, seeds, and fresh mint leaves on top for additional nutrients.

If you want a thicker smoothie that, for instance, could be poured into a bowl and eaten with a spoon, simply add more oats/banana.

I really like coconut milk in this smoothie but you can use any that you like. They all taste good!

This can be made in advance and stored in the fridge for up to 3 days. Alternatively, it will be perfect frozen for several months. Just defrost it at room temperature before putting it back in the blender and whizzing it up again before consuming.

**Note: This one is "Hugo Approved."
My six-year-old grandson loves this!**

 Prep Time
7 Minutes

 Cook Time
None

Super Green Energy Smoothie

Breakfast. Snack. Pre and Post workout. In fact, just enjoy anytime!
Food Heart: Fruits. Raw. Non-Starchy. Starchy. Nuts. Seeds. Healthy Fats.

Ingredients

- 1 green apple
- 1 ripe banana
- half a small pineapple
- 1 stick of celery
- 1 inch piece of ginger
- big handful of fresh spinach
- palmful of walnuts
- 1 tbsp hemp seeds (opt)
- Juice of fresh lime
- 250ml water / non-dairy milk
- ice cubes

Utensils

- Blender
- Chopping board
- Knife

Instructions

Halve then quarter the apple. Remove the core/seeds.

Roughly chop all the ingredients then place them all in the blender with your lime juice and water or non-dairy milk.

Blitz till smooth and creamy.

Decant into a glass or bowl.

If you want a thicker smoothie that could be poured into a bowl and eaten with a spoon simply add another banana.

I prefer water in this smoothie as I can then really taste all the flavours. It's great for digestion with the pairing of celery, pineapple, and ginger.

It can be made in advance and stored in the fridge for up to 3 days. Alternatively, it will be perfect frozen for several months. Just defrost it at room temperature before putting it back in the blender and whizzing it up again before consuming.

Prepare Time
5 Minutes

Cook Time
None

Mixed Berry Muffins

Breakfast. Snack. Sweet treat.

Food Heart: Berries. Fruits. Starchy. Healthy fats.

Ingredients

- 180g oat flour *
- 1 tsp baking powder
- 1 can cannellini beans
- 1 tsp ginger powder
- 1 tbsp Maple or M-Apple syrup
- 30g ground flaxseed
- 300g mixed fresh berries of your choice
- 1 ripe banana
- 2 tbsp unsweetened applesauce **

Utensils

- Mixing Bowl
- Muffin tray and cases
- Blender or food processor
- Chopping Board
- Knife
- Wire cooling tray

Instructions

Pop your oven on to 180 °C.

Line a muffin tray with 12 small or 9 large muffin cases.

Sieve the flour, ginger, and baking powder into a bowl.

Drain and rinse the cannellini beans, then put them in the blender or processor together with the flaxseed, banana, applesauce, syrup, and one third of the berries.
Blitz till you get a smooth batter.

Pour the batter into the bowl of dry ingredients and mix till well combined.

Add in the remaining berries, gently fold in.

Fill each muffin liner two thirds of the way up and place in oven for approx. 20 to 30 mins.

Tip: These are best served warm. I find that they microwave well in around 15 seconds from the fridge. They can also be frozen and will keep for a few months.
Defrost at room temperature, then warm in the microwave

* Blitz 180g whole oats into your blender or processor to make your own oat flour.
** Use an extra banana if you don't have applesauce.

Prep Time
10 Minutes

Cook Time
20–30 minutes

03 All day bites and mains

Lunch, dinner, mains, snacks, supper

Ever since I started on my plant-based eating journey, the differentiation between the standard meal times have pretty much dissipated. Apart from maybe breakfast because, as the name suggests, it's still that first meal you have in order to break the fast.

Once that's done, for the rest of my eating day I focus on two factors:

a) eating when I'm genuinely hungry (that can be any time of day or night),
b) filling my plate with as many nutrients as possible.

I don't have standard or regular eating times; with the busy and varied lifestyle that I lead, that just doesn't work for me.

When thinking about your own eating style, do what supports you and your lifestyle. It could be that the trad 'BLD' (Breakfast, Lunch, Dinner) suits your lifestyle and hunger times perfectly.

Or perhaps, like me, eating like a grazer at more random times of the day and night is a better fit.

There's no right or wrong way; your body will tell you exactly what it needs, and when it needs it.

Lunch, dinner, mains, snacks, supper

With this in mind, I've put together a range of dishes that all go towards making up a nutrient-dense, low (empty) calorie bowl or plate of food that will work for any time of the day or night.

Let's start by seeing how we put a plate together that will hit as many nutrients, fibre, and protein goals as possible, all in one delicious meal.

04   Be Nourished Bowl

Ingredients

Raw Salad
Non Starchy
Starchy
Fruit
Berries
Healthy Fats
Super Nutrient Sprinkle
(flaxseed, chia, hemp)

WHAT IS IT?

A **BE NOURISHED BOWL** is a nutrient dense meal all on one plate.

P.S. You can use any receptacle you want—a bowl, a plate, a box, a jar; whatever you have to hand!

It's really easy to put a Be Nourished Bowl together by using the good food heart as a guide.

The biggest proportion will be the raw salad element. Aim for 50%.

This will include leaves such as rocket, iceberg, romaine, spinach and micro-greens. Every different type of lettuce and leafage contains many different nutrients. Generally, green is the most nutrient dense but you should include every colour you can as all of these contain their own unique and vital nutrients.

Next, add in some non starchy foods. These include items such as cauliflower, broccoli, raw carrots, celeriac, asparagus, green beans, cucumber, mushrooms, tomatoes, beets, radishes, leeks, onions, peppers, sugar snaps to name just a few. These are great as part of your raw salad too. Win win! Aim for a good 25% here.

Already you have 75% of your bowl made up!

Now we can add some starchy items in. 15%.
This is where we include items such as chickpeas or beans. There are so many varieties of beans available, each offering their own range of protein and nutrients. We have pinto, borlotti, butter, cannellini, adzuki, black turtle, kidney.
If beans are not floating your taste boat, then you could opt for lentils, barley, millet or peas.
Throw in some steamed sweet potato, parsnip, or butternut squash and you have a great selection of healthy starches.

The final proportion of the plate can be made up of healthy fats, such as avocado, or perhaps a good handful of assorted nuts and seeds. I particularly love walnuts, sunflower and pumpkin seeds.
Add in a handful of berries with a tablespoon of ground flaxseed and you've got not only a nutrient-dense packed plate but also a whole rainbow of colours and textures that look and taste amazing.

Finish with an oil free mango, chilli, and lime dressing and voila! You have a complete
Be Nourished Bowl fit for a dinner party.

The Be Nourished Bowl, Deconstructed

Now that we know how a **Be Nourished Bowl** is put together, let's have a look at some individual recipes that all go towards creating your complete nutrient daily plates.

The biggest proportion of the food we consume should be **raw salad**. Why raw? The reason for eating raw is to obtain the highest density and quality of nutrients.

As soon as we begin to cook anything, the process of heating, particularly to high temperatures such as deep fat frying or oven roasting, cooking in water, or microwaving all lead to a loss of vital nutrients, being lost in the waters used to boil or destroyed by heating too high.

Tip: Don't boil; gently steam and leave food "al dente"

Be as creative as you want with your salads!

Include as many items as you like to get the max nutrition in your bowl: leaves, berries, grains, vegetables, mushrooms, onions, herbs.
Anything and everything that floats your boat can be put into a salad.

It's the main dish; the centerpiece of every meal, so indulge your palette and go all out.

LENTIL FLATBREADS

These are a super healthy alternative to bread and they go perfectly with walnut and spinach pesto or avocado tomato lime mix.

I love them for a lunch or as a snack when I'm busy and haven't got time to make up a big plate.

These flatbreads will keep in the fridge for a good five days or in the freezer for several months so they're great to make ahead of time.

Instructions

Place the lentils into a jug or jar large enough to hold 500 ml of water.
Cover them with water; I use double the amount of water to lentils so for 100g of lentils add 200ml of water.

If you are adding in any additional spices or seaweeds, now is the time to add them. Give it all a good stir so it's nicely combined.
Place them in the fridge overnight, or at least 4 hours to give them time to soak up the liquid.

I check the lentils after an hour or two and add more water if they've soaked it up already. Around half an inch of water above the lentils is enough. Too much water will make the batter too runny.

When you're ready to use, if you're baking on a flat sheet in the oven, pre-heat it to approx 180 °C. Cover a baking sheet with parchment.

If you decide to fry them on the hob, get your frying pan ready and brush it with a tiny bit of oil if it isn't nonstick.

Decant the lentils straight into the blender cup and blitz until smooth and resembles a batter.

Either pour on to the baking sheet, or heat up the frying pan and pour enough to cover the bottom of the pan.

Oven bake for approx 15 mins, then turn over and bake a further 10 mins. Remove from heat, let cool, then cut into pieces ready for your desired topping!

If frying, fry on one side till the edges are crispy and the mix is set enough to turn, then fry on the other side. These make great wraps as they hold together well.

Ingredients

- 100g red split lentils
- Enough water to cover the lentils around 200ml
- The following are all optional:
- 1 tsp smoked paprika
- 1 tsp turmeric
- 1 tsp cayenne
- A pinch of white pepper
- 1 tbsp nori or dulse seaweed flakes
- A large piece of irish moss seaweed

Equipment

- Blender
- Jug
- Frying pan or baking sheet
- Parchment paper
- Container to store flatbreads

AVOCADO, CHILLI, & LIME TOPPER

Ingredients
- 1 ripe avocado
- 1 garlic clove
- Handful mixed cherry tomatoes
- 1 lime, juice of
- 1 tsp paprika
- 1 tsp chilli flakes
- 1 spring onion, sliced thinly

Equipment
- Chopping board
- Knife
- Citrus juicer (optional)
- Spoon
- Fork
- Bowl

Prep Time
10 Minutes

Eat with
Lentil Flatbreads

Instructions

There's no point having a lentil flatbread if you've got nothing to put on it. My 'go-to' topper remains the same; a zingy avocado, chilli, and lime mix!

It's super easy to make. Simply cut the avocado in half, remove the stone, scoop out the flesh, and smash it up with a fork.

Prepare your garlic. Remove the hard end, place the flat of the knife over the top of the clove and smash it down with the palm of your hand.

This removes the skin easily.

Now slice it and dice it as finely as you can.

Wash the cherry tomatoes, halve them. If they are quite big, quarter them.

Wash the spring onion, remove the root end and the top dark green stems. Slice it thinly. I like to slice diagonally so it looks prettier.

Add your chilli flakes, spices, and lime juice to the avocado. Mix well.

Now add in your tomatoes and spring onion. Use a fork for this, taking care not to smash up the tomatoes too much.

Spread liberally on toasted lentil flatbreads, with a squeeze of fresh lime over the top.

This will keep two to three days covered in the fridge. I've never tried to freeze it as it never lasts that long, however I'm pretty sure it would be fine for a month or two in a suitable freezer container.

05 Oil Free Dressings & Pesto

Eat wholefood for health

MANGO CHILLI LIME SALAD DRESSING

Instructions

Peel the Mango.

I use my vegetable peeler for this.

Using a sharp knife, score the flesh into cubes, passing the flat of the knife blade underneath the cubes straight into the blender cup.

Mangoes have a large flat stone inside them and you'll find a lot of flesh will cling to it.

Now add the remainder of the ingredients into the blender cup and blitz on high for 1 min.

If the consistency is too thick, add a little more water till the desired consistency, pouring, is achieved.

Decant the dressing into a jar with a lid. Keep in the fridge for up to 5 days.

Alternatively, decant into a freezer container and freeze for several months.

Trust me, this dressing is so delicious, you won't be able to keep it that long!

I drizzle it over my salads to add a beautiful zingy kick.

Ingredients

- One Mango
- Chilli Flakes 1 tsp
- Garlic powder 1 tsp
- Juice of 1 lime
- Apple cider vinegar 100 ml
- Water 200 ml

Equipment

- Blender
- Jar to store dressing
- Vegetable peeler

Prepare Time
15 minutes

Blend Time
1 minute

WALNUT & WILTED SPINACH PESTO

Prepare Time
15 Minutes

Blend Time
2 Minutes

Serve with
Everything!

Instructions

Half fill your pan with boiling water.

Pop the colander on top and put the spinach into the colander. Place the lid over this so the steam doesn't escape.

Steam till the leaves are nicely wilted.

While the spinach is wilting, prepare the rest of the ingredients.

Garlic. Take the hard ends off, then place the flat of the knife over the top of the garlic clove and bash down sharply with your palm.
This will lift the skin off easily.

Pop all the ingredients except for the spinach and basil, if using, into the blender or chopper and blitz till a bread crumb consistency forms.

Now add a good ladle of the waters from the steamed spinach, together with the spinach and basil.

Blitz till combined and vibrant green. Add more steamed waters till you reach the consistency you prefer.

Decant into an airtight container. This will keep in the fridge up to 3 days or in the freezer for several months.

Ingredients

- 3 palmfuls sunflower seeds
- 3 palmfuls pumpkin seeds
- 1 palmful raw unsalted walnuts
- 2–4 garlic cloves
- 1 bag fresh spinach
- 2 tbsp nutritional yeast flakes
- 1 tbsp Nori or dulse seaweed flakes
- Boiling water to steam spinach
- Fresh basil, a few leaves (optional)

Equipment

- Blender
- Jar to store pesto
- Chopping board
- Knife
- Pot with lid
- Colander

Pesto Tips

Walnut and wilted spinach is by far my favourite pesto! I make it every single week and serve it with anything and everything.

The colour is a beautiful vibrant green and the flavour is so intense and fresh.

It's a great way of adding more nutrients, fibre, and protein to your daily plate and there are plenty of ways you can enjoy it as it's so versatile and pairs well with most other foods.

A delicious way to serve it is to fill a large field or portobello mushroom with a good heaped teaspoon of it then it can be air fried or oven baked. Just add a little water, there's no need for any oil.

Cook for around 15 mins till the mushroom is tender and juicy then simply eat as it is or, for additional nutrients, add a good handful of micro greens to the top.

It's a great bite to have on the side of your main meal.

Another way to serve it is just to add a teaspoon of it with your main dish.

Pop it on top of your soup, casserole, or salad, or thin it down and use it to coat your healthy pasta.

I love the Zen B range of pastas that are made with 100% yellow split peas.

All of the fibre, protein, nutrition, and taste with none of the guilt or bloat!

06 Let's get starchy!

So far so good! You're doing well.

You now have some easy breakfast ideas to get you revved up and raring to embrace your day, whatever time your day may start at.

You understand how to put a plate of nourishment together, as shown in the "Be Nourished Bowl" section.

By using all the food categories you know you've covered your fibre, protein, and nutrients for the day and, you've even had a lesson or two in making super healthy, lovely oil free dressings that will add the zing! to that Be Nourished Bowl.

The following recipes are ideas of how to add vital starchy foods as well as non-starchy, nuts, seeds, fruits, berries, and healthy fats as accompaniments to that rainbow salad and dressings.

A typical "**main**" meal for me looks a bit like this:
Half my plate is the **raw salad**; this includes **berries**, **nuts** and **seeds** as well as a big spoon of fresh **avocado**

Accompanied by:

A pesto-filled and air-fried field mushroom
Bowl of homemade soup or dahl
Lentil and seaweed flatbreads to dip and mop with

I batch make the soups and dahls, freezing portions down so I have a ready-made healthy microwave meal any day of the week and any time of the day.

Once you get the hang of thinking about your food in this new way, you'll come up with all your own recipes and dishes.

As I mentioned at the beginning, a recipe is just a guide, there to be tweaked and moulded the way you like best.

This recipe is going to make you happy!
One set of ingredients that makes two separate and equally delicious dishes.
Plus, all the ingredients are common pantry items and readily available in your local supermarket.

Ingredients

- 100g green lentils
- 50g oat flour *
- 3 to 4 medium mushrooms
- 2 medium carrots
- 2 sticks celery
- 1 large onion
- 4 garlic cloves
- 2 tbsp tomato puree
- 1 tbsp balsamic vinegar
- 1 tsp each: oregano, thyme, turmeric, cayenne
- 1 tsp miso paste

Equipment

- Chopping board
- Knife
- Large frying pan or wok
- Baking sheet
- Parchment paper
- Food Processor (optional)

Prepare Time

20 Minutes

Cook Time

35 to 40 Minutes

- *Tip: for oat flour, use whole gf oats and mill down in a food processor*

Instruction

First, rinse off the lentils under cold water. Place them in a pan and cover with double the amount of water. I like to add in some spices at this point so that the lentils absorb them during the cooking process, adding more flavour. Turn the hob onto med-high, bring to a boil, then turn right down and let simmer till the liquid is absorbed and the lentils are still slightly al dente. Remove from heat and let cool while you prepare the rest of the ingredients.

Wipe the mushrooms and wash the celery and carrots. Finely chop them all. There is no need to peel the carrots; the most nutrient dense part lies just under the skin. Same with the mushrooms, just wipe the skin with a dry piece of kitchen towel leaving the skin with all the nutrition intact. Chopping is much easier and quicker in a Ninja chopper than by hand but either is fine. Peel and finely chop the garlic and onion. Again in a Ninja chopper is easiest.

Set a large wok or frying pan on the hob to med heat. Add in the carrots with some water or stock and saute off for a few minutes. Add in the rest of the vegetables and mushrooms as well as all the spices, balsamic, tomato puree, herbs, and miso paste. Wait 5 minutes till softened.

Add in the lentils and the oat flour. I combine everything in the wok but you can pop it all in a food processor and pulse it all to combine.

Chill for 30 mins in the fridge, then shape into burgers or balls. I set these freshly formed burgers or balls onto a baking sheet covered with fresh parchment paper, then put back in the fridge for a further 15 to 20 minutes.

The additional time in the fridge will set the mixture and help them keep their shape once you pop them in the oven.

Cook for approximately 20 mins till slightly browned and crisp on the outside.

Both versions can be kept in the fridge for up to 5 days or wrapped and put in the freezer for several months.

TIPS:
Instead of a bread bap for the burger version, try sitting the burger in a lentil wrap, on a crunchy romaine lettuce leaf, or even a large field mushroom.

Make a sausage shape instead of the burger or balls and use as part of a healthy vegan no oil fry up. Perfect for that slow Sunday morning!

The recipe for the sauce part of the Saucy Balls follows next.

HERBY TOMATO SAUCE

Ingredients

- 800g fresh or 2 tins of chopped tomatoes
- 3 garlic cloves, peeled
- 2 tbsp nutritional yeast flakes
- 1 tbsp tomato puree
- 1 tbsp tahini paste
- 1 tsp smoked paprika
- 1 tsp cayenne
- 1 tsp turmeric
- 1 tsp dried thyme
- 1 tsp dried basil
- 1 tsp dried oregano

Equipment

- Chopping board
- Knife
- Blender
- Jar for storing sauce

Prepare Time
5 Minutes

Cook Time
10 Minutes

Instructions

Place all ingredients in the blender and blitz on full till smooth. Keep in a jar in the fridge till you want to use it. Place in a pan with the lentil balls and warm gently on the hob medium heat for 5 to 10 mins. The sauce freezes and defrosts perfectly.

RED LENTIL & SWEET POTATO DAHL

Ingredients

- 3 white onions, chopped
- 6 garlic cloves, peeled and smashed
- 2 sweet potatoes
- 1 small butternut squash
- 1 tbsp ground cumin
- 1 tsp ground coriander
- 1 tsp turmeric
- 1 tsp miso paste
- 200g red split lentils
- 250g bag fresh spinach
- Punnet cherry tomatoes

Equipment

- Chopping board
- Knife
- Veg peeler
- 5-litre pan for hob

Prepare Time

20 Minutes

Cook Time

25 Minutes

Instructions

This is a beautiful fragrant and filling dish; easy to prepare and can be made in big batches giving you an opportunity to portion some out to be kept in the freezer, ready for those evenings when you come home late, too tired to cook from scratch. Reach into your freezer and voila! You have a healthy, tasty microwave meal, ready in a jiffy.

Prepare all your ingredients: peel the sweet potato and butternut squash. Cube the butternut in small bite size pieces and roughly chop the sweet potato into much larger pieces. Sweet potato doesn't take long to cook and will break down quickly once it has cooked through. Butternut takes longer to cook and will retain its texture even after cooking. Peel and roughly chop both the onion and garlic.

Add both to the pan, set on a med-high heat. Cover with water. Pop lid on and let this simmer till softened. Keep adding bits of water (or stock) to prevent sticking and burning. Once softened, add the spices and mix in well.

Add in the butternut and cook this for a good 5 minutes till it starts to go soft; add in the sweet potato and cherry tomatoes. Top up with water or stock so all the vegetables are covered. Bring to a boil, turn the heat down, and simmer for 10 minutes. Now add the lentils and simmer away for another 10 to 15 minutes till everything is cooked through and the lentils are pale and breaking down.

Turn the heat off and add the spinach so it wilts in the heat, then ladle into a bowl with a teaspoon of pesto and some chunks of lentil flatbread.

GAZPACHO

Ingredients

- 4–5 beef tomatoes, roughly chopped
- 3–4 garlic cloves, peeled and smashed
- 2 romero pepper, remove stalk and seeds, roughly chop
- 1 medium brown onion, peeled, and roughly chopped
- 1 small cucumber, peeled, and roughly chopped
- 1 tsp ground cumin
- 1 tsp turmeric
- 1 tsp miso paste
- 1 tbsp balsamic vinegar
- 1 tbsp tahini paste (opt)

Equipment

- Chopping board
- Knife
- Vegetable peeler
- Blender

Instructions

- Add all ingredients to a blender
- Blitz on high speed till a smooth consistency is achieved
- Add water if you want thinner consistency

Prepare Time
20 Minutes

Cook Time
None!

Tip
Make a large batch and freeze in individual portions.
Keeps in fridge 3 to 5 days.

GREEN GAZPACHO

Ingredients

- 1 large cucumber, peel and rough chop
- 3–4 garlic cloves, peeled and smashed
- 1 large head of broccoli, rough chop
- 1 medium brown onion, peeled and rough chopped
- 2 tbsp nutritional yeast flakes
- 1 handful fresh mint leaves, rough chop
- 1 tsp cayenne (opt)
- 1 tsp miso paste
- 1 lemon; juice and grated zest
- 1 tbsp tahini paste (opt)

Equipment

- Chopping board
- Knife
- Blender

Instructions

- Add all ingredients to a blender.
- Blitz on high speed till a smooth consistency is achieved.
- Add water if you want thinner consistency.

Prepare Time

20 Minutes

Cook Time

None!

Tip

Make a large batch and freeze in individual portions.
Keeps in fridge 3 to 5 days.
I like to add a tbsp of white beans to the soup.

07 Not So Naughty Sweetie

Eat sweet from Natures Orchard

Sweet, Creamy, Gooey, Dreamy . . . those words conjure up visions of sweet sugary delights, as well as a huge sigh and recognition that you can't have too much of a good thing so we'd best make that portion a small please.

But wait . . . that's actually not true! One of the best things I discovered through eating plant-based was that I could find so many ways to sate my liking for sweet, creamy, colourful desserts just by using basic everyday ingredients in ways I didn't realise I could.

I've popped together a couple of not so naughty sweet treats so you can give this a go yourself!

No Guilt Nice Cream

Ingredients

- 2 large frozen bananas
- 100 ml coconut milk
- 1 tbsp peanut butter
- 1 tsp vanilla essence
- 1 tbsp chia seeds or ground chia
- 1 handful crushed walnuts to garnish (opt)

Equipment

- Chopping board
- Knife
- Blender

Instructions

- Pre-Prep: Cut your over ripened bananas into chunks. Pop in freezer bag or container and freeze for a minimum of 4 hours. When ready to use, there is no need to defrost, just put the frozen fruit straight into the blender!
- Add all ingredients to a blender.
- Blitz on high speed till a smooth consistency is achieved.
- Decant into a bowl, sprinkle with walnuts and eat straight away.

Prep Time

4 hours to freeze fruits then 5 minutes to make straight from the freezer!

Cook Time

None!

Tip

Adding a couple of tablespoons of soft silken tofu will make this nice cream even creamier and smoother. In fact, it gives it a lovely glossy "silken" finish!

Berry Lovely Smoothie Bowl

Ingredients

- 100g whole oats
- 150 ml coconut milk
- 1 banana
- 4 fresh strawberries
- 1 tbsp peanut butter
- 1 tsp vanilla essence
- 1 tbsp chia seeds or ground chia
- 300g fresh or frozen berries of your choice
- 1 tbsp pea protein (opt)

Equipment

- Chopping board
- Knife
- Blender
- 2 bowls

Instruction

- Add all the ingredients except the berries into the blender.
- Blitz on high speed till a smooth consistency is achieved.
- Decant into two bowls.
- Decorate with the berries and eat straight away.

Prep Time

10 minutes

Cook Time

None!

Tip

You can mill your oats down in a high powered blender to make them finer. The finished smoothie bowl will be much . . . smoother!

Healthy Sugar Free Granola

Ingredients
- 150g mixed raw nuts and seeds
- 150g oats (GF if possible)
- 100g cocoa butter drops or coconut oil, melted
- 1 tbsp tahini (opt)
- 1 tbsp maple syrup
- 1 tsp vanilla essence
- 1 tsp each ground cinnamon and ginger

Instruction
- Pre-heat oven to 170°C / 340°F
- Line a baking sheet with parchment paper.
- Melt the cocoa drops or coconut oil either in the microwave or in a glass bowl over a pan of water.
- Pulse the nuts and seeds till they're broken into small pieces; put in bowl with the rest of the dry ingredients.
- Combine the wet and dry ingredients, coating well.
- Spread out on baking sheet, put in oven for 20–30 mins till golden brown.
- Let cool before decanting into the Kilner jar.
- Store for up to 4 weeks, if you can keep them that long!

Prep Time
10 minutes

Cook Time
30 minutes

Equipment
- Ninja Chopper
- Bowl
- Baking sheet
- Kilner Jar

Tip
I love pumpkin and sunflower seeds with a mix of walnut, brazil, and cashew nuts.

Double Trouble Chocolate Avocado

Ingredients:

Chocolate Avocado Layer

- 4 medium ripe avocados
- 60g cocoa powder
- 60g melted raw vegan chocolate
- 1 tbsp tahini (opt)
- 60 ml maple syrup
- 50 ml aquafaba
- 50 ml oat or coconut milk
- 1 tbsp silken tofu
- 1 tsp coffee

Peanut Butter Mousse Layer

- 260g raw unsalted peanut butter
- 260g vegan cream cheese *
- 230ml double cream **
- 1 tbsp tahini (opt)
- 120ml maple syrup
- 1 tsp vanilla essence
- 1 tbsp silken tofu (opt)
- 50ml aquafaba
- */** See "instruction" sheet for details and tips

Equipment

- Electric whisk and blender
- Bowl, knife, and chopping board
- Spoon and 10 glass ramekin dishes, or similar

Prep Time
40 minutes

Cook Time
Leave overnight to set.

Topping

Anything you like!
I chose frozen raspberries, crumbled up with crushed pecan nuts finely chopped fresh pears tumbled over the top.

To finish, I fine grated some dark chocolate over the dish. This dessert has been my most popular to date!

Instructions

This is a sumptuous and decadent dessert with aesthetics that has got "**naughty**" written all over it!

However, when you check out those ingredients, you will note that rather than being full of heavy creams, calorie dense chocolates, and stacked full of refined sugars, this dessert is remarkably free from the baddies.

What better way to wow your guests at a dinner party, or just pure old self indulge on a cosy winters night, with a great romcom and toasting your toes in front of the log burner than with a very much "**not so naughty, sweetie**" dessert.

To make the **chocolate avocado** base layer, first warm the milk in the microwave and stir in the teaspoon of coffee till dissolved.

Next, scoop the flesh out of the avocados and place it, along with all the other ingredients EXCEPT for the raw chocolate, into the blender jug and blitz till smooth and creamy.

Melt the chocolate in the microwave. If you prefer, you can put the chocolate into a glass bowl; half fill a pan with hot water then set the glass bowl on top of the pan. Set the hob to a medium heat and melt the chocolate this way.

Now pour the melted chocolate into the blender and pulse till combined. Decant into the ramekins to the halfway point. Pop in fridge for minimum 30 mins to set.

To make the **peanut butter mousse** layer, decant the double cream into a bowl and whisk up till stiff peaks form. Set aside. Put all the remaining ingredients into the blender jug and blitz till smooth and creamy. Now, remove the blade and gently fold in the whipped cream.

This can be either piped on top of the chocolate avocado layer or spooned on. Pop in fridge for a minimum of 3 hours or, ideally, overnight.

Decorate with your chosen toppings just before serving.

- *You can buy vegan cream cheese from the supermarket or you can easily make your own cream cheese using cashews. I prefer making my own as I then know exactly what's in it. You can learn how easy it is to make basic cheeses on my cook and eat workshops.

- **My preferred vegan double cream is **Oatly**. I find it whips up the best and in the quickest time! *NB, I am not affiliated to any brand, therefore I do not make any commission from any brand that I may mention.*

This keeps well, covered, in the fridge for 3 to 4 days.
Due to the avocado and raw nuts, this dessert is full of healthy fibres, fats, and protein!

Butterfly Blue Pea Flower tea

I'm sure you've all seen or had the delectable butterfly blue pea flower tea.

Not only is it the most beautiful vibrant blue when steeped, it's packed full of great nutrients and is thought to be amazing for promoting and regulating mental well-being; it's known as the "brain herb" and is used to treat symptoms of depression and anxiety.

My grandson loves it in a banana, blueberry, and oat milk smoothie. Pop the fruit and milk in the blender while steeping a heaped teaspoon of blue pea flower in hot water. Once fully steeped, add the water to the blender, add a teaspoon of chia seeds, blitz till smooth, creamy and vibrant blue, pour, then simply sip and savour.

The Gibson

What better way to finish your kick start journey into easy everyday plant-based eating than with a cool glass of gin!

This is how you make a Gibson:

1 measure of Gin, London Dry
2 small pickled onions
1 tbsp pickle juice
Ice

Add all the above to a glass. Drink. Enjoy. Cheers!

The Gibson comes courtesy of Nick, an old favourite from his college days in Chicago.

I hope you've enjoyed my recipes as much as I've loved sharing them. If you have any questions or need help with your diet, you can find me at

www.benourished.im

To your best health, always

"Your health is your first foundation"

Take care of your body; it is, after all, the only vehicle you get to own, the only vessel you'll use to explore the world and the only house you can ever truly call a home.

Steven Bartlett
The Diary of a CEO

Medical Disclaimer

The information contained in this book are my thoughts, ideas, and personal experiences around food, nutrition, and wellness and hence, all information presented is for informational purposes only.

The information in this book is not intended to diagnose, treat, cure, or prevent any disease and is not intended to be a replacement for any medical treatment.

This book is not intended to be used for therapeutic purposes, as medical advice, or to offer a cure to any health or medical condition nor intends to provide a substitute for the advice provided by a physician or other healthcare professional.

If you are pregnant, nursing, have a medical condition or are taking any ongoing medication, please seek the advice of your healthcare practitioner before making any changes to your diet, lifestyle, or supplement regime.

Please always seek the advice of a healthcare practitioner for your specific health concerns.

© 2024

MEET THE AUTHOR

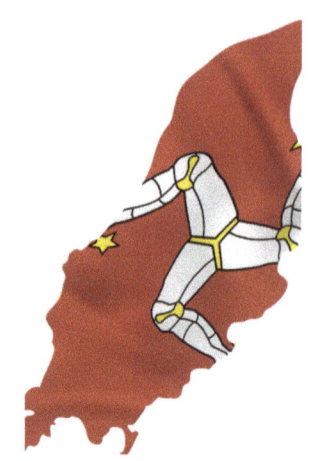

Born, raised, and educated on the Isle of Man, where she was surrounded by an abundance of foods growing readily in the **fields, glens, and hedgerows**, Michelle Garrett-Chambers learned a fundamental truth very early: that the best food comes naturally, pulled directly from the earth.

This love of real food, passed
down to her by her grandparents, stayed with her.
And as the connection between processed foods and poor health has grown more apparent, the lessons of her youth feel more important than ever.
Fuelled by the knowledge gained from her **roots**, and armed with the wisdom handed down through the generations, Michelle now works to give everyone the ability to feed themselves well without the confusion that surrounds so much of what we eat, and how, in the modern world.

Dedicating her life to researching **plant-based nutrition**, she now works to educate others and drive
change in the ways in which we think about food and our relationship to nature.

www.ingramcontent.com/pod-product-compliance
Lightning Source LLC
Chambersburg PA
CBHW060935170426
43194CB00026B/2965